Journal of Beat Studies

Volume 7, 2019

PACE UNIVERSITY PRESS • NEW YORK

Copyright © 2019 by
Pace University Press
41 Park Row, 15th Floor
New York, NY 10038

All rights reserved
Printed in the United States of America

ISSN 2165-8706
ISBN: 978-1-935625-38-4 (pbk: alk.ppr.)

Member

Council of Editors of Learned Journals

♾ Paper used in this publication meets the minimum requirements of
American National Standard for Information
Sciences–Permanence of Paper for Printed Library Materials,
ANSI Z39.48–1984

Editors

Ronna C. Johnson — Tufts University
Nancy M. Grace — The College of Wooster (emerita)

Book Review Editor

Matt Theado — Kobe City University of Foreign Sudies (Kobe, Japan)

Editorial Board

Ann Charters — University of Connecticut–Storrs (emerita)
Maria Damon — Pratt Institute of Art
Terence Diggory — Skidmore College (emeritus)
Tim Gray — CUNY Staten Island
Oliver Harris — Keele University, United Kingdom
Allen Hibbard — Middle Tennessee State University
Tim Hunt — Illinois State University
A. Robert Lee — The University of Murcia, Spain
Cary Nelson — University of Illinois
Jennie Skerl — West Chester University (retired)
David Sterritt — Long Island University (emeritus)
Tony Trigilio — Columbia College–Chicago
John Tytell — CUNY Queens College
John Whalen-Bridge — National University of Singapore, Singapore

Production Staff

Stephanie Hsu — Production Editor, Pace University Press
Jessica Estrella — Graduate Assistant, Pace University Press
Alicia Hughes — Graduate Assistant, Pace University Press

Journal of Beat Studies

Volume 7, 2019

	1	Letter from the Editors
Jean-Christophe Cloutier	5	Jack Kerouac's Love Affair with Libraries Le mal d'archive de Jack Kerouac Jack Kerouac's Archive Fever
Jonathan Sedberry	19	Virus and Word Virus: David Wojnarowicz, HIV/AIDS, and The Beat Generation

THE BEAT INTERVIEW

Ronna C. Johnson and Nancy M. Grace	33	Home Movies by Bobbie Louise Hawkins

REVIEWS

Allan Johnston	59	*The Cambridge Companion to the Beats* edited by Steven Belletto
Michael Amundsen	66	*Hip Sublime: Beat Writers and the Classical Tradition* edited by Sheila Murnaghan and Ralph M. Rosen
Chris Gair	71	*The Spiritual Imagination of the Beats* by David Stephen Calonne
Douglas Field	75	*The Routledge Handbook of International Beat Literature* edited by A. Robert Lee
Maria Damon	79	*Women Writers of the Beat Era: Autobiography and Intertextuality* by Mary Paniccia Carden

James Peacock	**84**	*Kerouac on Record: A Literary Soundtrack* edited by Simon Warner and Jim Sampas
John Whalen-Bridge	**88**	*Mountains, Rivers, and the Great Earth: Reading Gary Snyder and Dōgen in an Age of Ecological Crisis* by Jason M. Wirth
	93	The Beat Index
	110	Essay Abstracts
	111	Notes on Contributors
	113	Editorial Policy

Letter from the Editors

In this, the seventh issue of the *Journal of Beat Studies*, we're pleased to feature a long interview with Bobbie Louise Hawkins, who passed away in May 2018. Titled "Home Movies by Bobbie Louise Hawkins," it combines two interviews we conducted with her in 2001 and 2002. In these exchanges, Hawkins not only recapitulates her life history as a painter, writer, and instructor at the Jack Kerouac School of Disembodied Poetics, but also recounts how women artists worked amidst some of the major figures in mid-twentieth-century American literary movements, Beat generation and Beat-associated. Poet Anne Waldman had urged us to interview Hawkins, and we had hoped to include it in our book *Breaking the Rule of Cool* (2004), but that plan did not come to fruition. In the meantime, The Beat Studies Association entered into an arrangement with Pace University Press to publish the *Journal of Beat Studies,* and then we, as *Journal* editors, instituted the annual Beat Interview with issue No. 4 in 2016. When Hawkins died on May 4, 2018, in Boulder, Colorado, her warm and animated talk in the two interviews we had with her came immediately to mind as we planned to commemorate her, along with her close friend the poet Joanne Kyger, who died the year before. In *Breaking the Rule of Cool*, we had already brought out the 2002 interview with Kyger, but we still had the unpublished sessions with Hawkins in our files. Hearing her footloose voice through the interviews as she reminisced about her life and related her experiences as an emerging writer in the several overlapping art and literary communities to which she belonged from the 1970s until her death was inspiring. We thought that printing the two interviews would be a just way to celebrate Hawkins's too often unsung place in several significant postwar literary movements, events, and groups. We had made a contemporaneous typescript of the two interviews, so we had a vintage record of the talks. Indeed, Hawkins was "a talker," as her garrulity in the interviews attests. "Writing," she told us, "is a great thing for talkers. It's how you get to keep talking when nobody's there." Well, Hawkins is no longer "there," but we can read her work and we can hear her vivid voice, which she herself identified as a wellspring of her writing.

From the provinciality of small town Texas, Hawkins, eventually a novelist, poet, and teacher, traveled the continental United States and countries abroad, which provide the context for her anecdotes about the writers who became her friends when she was married to poet Robert Creeley. These stories testify to the power of arts communities to educate and nurture fledgling voices with the verve to survive and invent themselves as artists. And Hawkins's memories of her own efforts to develop as a writer, including the too-familiar story of a woman writing in secret, provide hope as well as viable composition strategies for anyone seeking or struggling to bring forth an authentic literary voice. We hope that returning here to Hawkins's life story and her provocative talking will carve out a space in Beat literary history for many other artists and readers to reflect on.

The issue also includes two essays. Jonathan Sedberry's study of Beat-influenced writer, visual artist, and AIDS activist David Wojnarowicz (1954–1992) explores the impact of William S. Burroughs, and to some extent Jack Kerouac, on Wojnarowicz's autobiography *Close to the Knives* (1991). Life writing in essay form, *Close to the Knives* is described by The Guardian as a "chopped up, collaged structure" that maps "a place of loss and danger, of transient beauty and dogged resistance."[1] Sedberry argues that although Burroughs did not directly address the HIV/AIDS plague, a seemingly perfect fit with his philosophy of Word Virus, he contributed to the HIV/AIDS canon through his inspiration of Wojnarowicz, whose art and writing countered in Burroughsian dissent the hateful homophobic rhetoric coloring the first decade of the epidemic.

In "Jack Kerouac's Love Affair with Libraries," a two-part essay in French and English subtitled "Le Mal d'Archive de Jack Kerouac" and "Jack Kerouac's Archive Fever," respectively, Jean-Christophe Cloutier discusses Kerouac's relationship to libraries, which the writer revealed in his journals and in the Duluoz Legend. As Cloutier wrote us, "In September 2015, I was invited by Élisabeth Nardout-Lafarge, professor in the Département des littératures de langue française at the Université de Montréal, to contribute a short piece on Kerouac for a retrospective focus on the Franco-American author in the Canadian literary magazine *Liberté*. The article was to have appeared alongside three other reflections in the 'Rétroviseur' [rear-view mirror] section of the magazine. Alas, one of the contributors fell through and the magazine was already suffering from multiple production delays," so the essay was newly available for publication. Cloutier then expanded the essay into the English translation for the *Journal of Beat Studies*. We thank him for working with us on this insightful exploration of the social and literary dimensions of Kerouac's history with libraries, including The Pollard Memorial Public Library in Lowell, Massachusetts, and The New York City Public Library.

The last year or so has seen a rich body of scholarly publications in the field of Beat studies, and some of these are reflected in our latest review offerings: Michael Amundsen on *The Hip Sublime: Beat Writers and the Classical Tradition* (The Ohio State University Press 2018), edited by Sheila Murnaghan and Ralph M. Rosen; Maria Damon on Mary Paniccia Carden's *Women Writers of the Beat Era: Autobiography and Intertextuality* (University of Virginia Press 2018); Douglas Field on *The Routledge Handbook of International Beat Literature* (Routledge 2018), edited by A. Robert Lee; Christopher Gair on *The Spiritual Imagination of the Beats* (Cambridge University Press 2017) by David Stephen Calonne; Allan Johnston on *The Cambridge Companion to the Beats* (Cambridge University Press 2017), edited by Steven Belletto; James Peacock on *Kerouac on Record: A Literary Soundtrack* (Bloomsbury Academic 2018), edited by Simon Warner and Jim Sampas; and John Whalen-Bridge on *Mountains, Rivers, and the Great Earth: Reading Gary Snyder and Dōgen in an Age of Ecological Crisis* by Jason M. Wirth (State University of New York Press 2017).

LETTER FROM THE EDITORS

The Beat Index rounds out the volume.

Finally, we thank a number of individuals who provided us with invaluable assistance: Stephanie Hsu, associate director of Pace University Press, for her hard work, high standards, and generous spirit; Kelly Watt, assistant director of marketing and admissions, Naropa University; Amanda Koob, director for library and archives, Naropa University; Peter Hale, of the Allen Ginsberg Estate; Sean Thibodeau, coordinator of community planning, Pollard Memorial Library, Lowell, Massachusetts; Alison Zaya, reference librarian, Pollard Memorial Public Library, Lowell, Massachusetts; Kathie Clyde, transcriber, Wooster, Ohio; Mary Nieneber Gadd, research assistant, Columbus, Ohio; and Elsa Dorfman, photographer and memoirist from Cambridge, Massachusetts, whose vintage pictures of her friend Bobbie Louise Hawkins—as well as other writers of the Beat generation available in *Elsa's Housebook*—gave the Beat Interview an inimitable personal vibe.

We hope you enjoy it.

Onward!
Ronna C. Johnson and Nancy M. Grace

Notes

[1] See https://www.theguardian.com/books/2016/may/13/david-wojnarowicz-close-to-the-knives-a-memoir-of-disintegration-artist-aids-activist).

Jack Kerouac's Love Affair with Libraries
Jean-Christophe Cloutier

Memorial Hall and Public Library in Lowell, Massachusetts, circa 1908 (courtesy of the Library of Congress).

Le mal d'archive de Jack Kerouac

Jack Kerouac aimait les bibliothèques. Quand il était petit, il lisait tous les livres qui se trouvaient dans la « cabane » ainsi que toute la paperasse que son père, imprimeur, ramenait chez eux.[1] Adolescent, il faisait souvent l'école buissonnière non pas (seulement) pour aller jouer des mauvais tours mais surtout pour se cacher dans un racoin de la bibliothèque publique de la ville de Lowell, au Massachusetts, et y lire toutes sortes de livres—philosophie, littérature, sports, stratégie d'échecs, n'importe quoi—en français et en anglais. Kerouac a même établi un record pour les absences de jours de classes au Lowell High School en 1939, et tout cela parce qu'il aimait trop lire! Cet engouement s'est poursuivi lors de ses études universitaires à Columbia, à New York, où il tomba littéralement en amour avec la New York Public Library. Celle-là même qui, aujourd'hui, a la responsabilité de son fonds d'archives.

Dans son journal intime de 1947, à l'âge de 25 ans, il compose un court texte intitulé « Sur les bibliothèques des grandes villes » :

> Les deux bibliothèques de grande ville que j'ai eu l'occasion de fréquenter, celle de Boston et l'autre plus grande de New York, m'ont toujours rempli d'un sentiment indicible de joie quand je m'y rends, une joie qui est

composée des différentes choses suivantes : voir des vieux bonhommes fous déambuler en profonde méditation, voir les pigeons dans la cour de la fenêtre des bécosses, voir des belles filles assises en train de lire, et finalement participer à un sentiment de jubilation générale que ceci est la « culture » de premier ordre et que ceux qui sont ici réunis sont tous des penseurs profonds invétérés. J'aime bien me faufiler partout comme un penseur fou avec mon manteau volant derrière moi.

Mais, Kerouac ajoute, « jamais n'ai-je écris une bonne ligne dans la bibliothèque. » [2] En effet pour le grand voyageur, la bibliothèque est un endroit de méditation, de pensées, une communauté culturelle de connaissance et de savoir, mais ce n'est pas un lieu où il peut créer son œuvre littéraire.

Et pourtant, l'idée des bibliothèques, des fiches, et des dossiers sont à la base de sa pensée et de sa relation avec la mémoire, et avec l'histoire. Dans *Visions of Cody*, il nous révèle que pendant son sommeil, son esprit tente sans cesse de créer de « belles combinaisons » en « rebrassant les vieilles fiches de l'âme » (15). Sa pensée est tellement associée à la matérialité de l'information organisée des bibliothèques qu'il se remémore ses souvenirs comme étant inscrits sur des fiches. Un peu plus tard dans le même roman, il confirme cette association en imaginant un rolodex de la mémoire : « suppose qu'à chaque fois que tu entends une idée délicieusement originale ou qu'il te soit donné une image qui fait chanter l'esprit, tu pourrais immédiatement la flanquer dans un de ces nouveaux classeurs rotatifs de bureaux » (39). Malgré ce fantasme et ses attentions au classement et à la classification, Kerouac sait bien cependant que la mémoire n'est pas aussi organisé qu'une archive et il est hanté par la spectralité de ses efforts, l'eros et thanatos de ce que Jacques Derrida appelle le « mal de l'archive. » [3] « Je suis conscient de ma propre tragédie personnelle, » Kerouac déclare, « ma chambre même en est hantée la nuit quand je dors ou me réveille, par une série d'images désespérées, me prenant soudainement en train de brasser les fiches de la mémoire ou de l'esprit par en-dessous du paquet » (*Cody* 41). Sa plus grande peur, il continue, serait de « jeter quelque chose que je n'arrive même pas à trouver dans le désordre incroyable de mon être mais qui est en voie de s'échapper avec le détritus en masse, enseveli dans le milieu, de temps en temps je l'aperçois » (42). Kerouac décrit ainsi son mal d'archive, cette souffrance, cette passion qui le pousse non seulement à parcourir ses fiches de mémoire mais aussi les grands chemins de l'Amérique. Pour Derrida, ce mal de l'archive : « C'est n'avoir de cesse, interminablement, de chercher l'archive là où elle se dérobe. C'est courir après elle là où, même s'il y en a trop, quelque chose en elle s'anarchive » (Derrida 142). Le tout résonne avec une ressemblance incroyable, comme une incarnation de ce que Kerouac exprime dans son oeuvre : « de temps en temps, » il dit arriver à apercevoir, et ce à l'endroit même où un « trop » de fiches en désordre se présente, l'archive qui se dérobe dans le détritus, s'anarchive vers l'oubli. Voilà ce qui nous aide à comprendre non seulement la montagne immense de mots que Kerouac a réussi à coucher sur papier durant ses 47 ans de vie, mais aussi son affinité et son appréciation pour les méthodes de conservation du passé qui se trouvent dans ces temples de la mémoire que nous appelons les bibliothèques.

La relation que Kerouac entretient avec les bibliothèques évolue avec les années. Quelques notes écrites en août 1951 nous présentent un Kerouac qui se souvient des heures qu'il a « passé dans la Lowell High School Library à lire les petits caractères de l'Encyclopédie Britannica (édition de 1911 en papier pelure) et plus tard dans la Horace Mann Library, celle qui avait du lierre en dehors de la fenêtre, » et en conclut que c'est grâce à ces heures qu'il en est venu à finalement comprendre ce qu'était les « jours gris » de la vie (JKP, 16.12). Un mois plus tard, en plein conflit intérieur avec sa « dualité Canuck de merde, » il écrit dans son journal : « L'esprit du *plaisir* venant des occupations solitaires est ce que je dois récupérer de l'enfance pour l'ouvrage artistique de l'âge adulte... l'énorme préoccupation de jours gris avec les fichiers, les dossiers, les systèmes, les petits caractères, histoires éculées dans des tomes poussiéreux » (Cloutier 47). Les « jours gris » sont donc une source de plaisir, et sa préoccupation des fichiers sera donc partie prenante de « l'ouvrage de sa vie. » Il faut souligner aussi que, dans le contexte historique des Canadiens français vivant aux États-Unis, cette préoccupation fait partie intégrante de ce que l'on appelait la survivance, soit cet effort de préserver son héritage, sa langue, et sa culture enfouie au centre du mouvement d'assimilation hostile vécu à l'époque.

Pourtant Kerouac finira par ne plus croire en son propre projet archivistique. Ses doutes referont surface un an plus tard, et il écrira dans son journal d'août 1952 : « je réalise que je n'ai pas besoin de continuer mon journal—pourquoi encombrer le monde avec mes mots de bagatelles quotidiennes, etc., ce sont les esquisses, les histoires et les romans de nouvelle-prose qui videront ma part des choses sales dans la boîte de la bibliothèque pour que les porcs les envalent toutes » (JKP, 15.12). En effet, au fil des ans, le mal d'archive de Kerouac devient de plus en plus problématique. Dans *Visions of Gerard*, écrit en 1956, il affirme directement que le mal s'est répandu : « I'm grown sick in my papers » (545). (Une phrase à temporalité double; en français, ce serait à la fois « je deviens » et « je suis devenu » « malade dans mes papiers »). Malgré tout, pendant son voyage en Europe en 1965, périple qu'il raconte dans le dernier extrait de la Légende de Duluoz, *Satori in Paris*, Kerouac cherche à retrouver les traces généalogiques de ses ancêtres français et bretons dans les grandes bibliothèques de Paris.

« J'essayais de trouver des choses à propos de ma vieille famille, » il nous raconte et rajoute, avec fierté, « J'étais le premier Lebris de Kérouack à retourner en France depuis 210 ans » (Satori 34-35). Malheureusement, dès son arrivée, Kerouac ne rencontre que des restrictions, des dossiers détruits, et des réactions peu encourageantes, terminant sa première journée à la Bibliothèque Nationale de France avec une plainte immature : « Tu peux pas fumer même aux toilettes à la Bibliothèque Nationale et tu ne peux même pas dire un mot avec toutes les secrétaires autour et il semble y avoir une fierté nationale à propos des « savants » qui sont tous assis-là en train de copier » (22). À sa deuxième journée, sa paranoïa s'amplifie, et il s'imagine que les gendarmes veulent « abattre ce rat du Québec » qu'il représente (30). Kerouac s'installe à une table de travail et trouve maintenant désagréable, contrairement à son expérience antérieure, l'environnement de la bibliothèque. C'est pourri « de milliers de chercheurs et des millions de livres et d'étranges bibliothécaires-adjointes […] qui admirent une belle *calligraphie* plus que n'importe quoi chez un chercheur ou un écrivain » (32). Les bibliothécaires se rendent compte rapidement que M. Kerouac avait bu : « Bien sûr, » Kerouac souligne, « ils ont tous senti l'alcool sur moi et me pensait fou » (32). Quand on lui demande de quitter les lieux, il se défend en expliquant qu'il « connaît les bibliothèques! » et, plus précisément, « la plus grande bibliothèque du monde, la New York Public Library, » et que donc il ne devrait « pas être regardé avec suspicion dans la Bibliothèque de Paris » (33). Son problème, pourrait-on dire, est qu'il est trop familier avec les bibliothèques; il s'y sent chez lui et se comporte en public comme on devrait seulement le faire en privé.

Plus tard, face à l'échec total de ses recherches dans les archives françaises, Kerouac semble perdre toute confiance de retrouver les traces de ses origines mais aussi avec tout projet archivistique. Sa dernière description de la Bibliothèque Nationale est comme un grand désaveu:

> La bibliothèque entière gémissait avec le débris accumulé de siècles de folie enregistrée, comme si t'avais besoin d'enregistrer la folie dans le Vieux ou le Nouveau Monde de toute manière, comme mon armoire chez nous avec le débris incroyable de vieilles lettres en désordre par milliers, de livres, de poussière, de magazines, de résultats de courses d'enfance, tel que quand je me suis réveillé l'autre nuit d'un sommeil pur, m'a fait gémir juste à penser que c'était ça ce à quoi j'avais passé mes heures éveillées : me bâdrer avec des bigotes que ni moi, ni personne d'autre voudrait ou ne pourrait vraiment se souvenir... (35)

Ce passage, tiré de la fin de la Légende, est une renonciation remarquable à tout ce que Kerouac avait jadis préconisé. L'histoire du monde et l'histoire privée de l'homme sont réduites ici à la folie, et l'habileté de pouvoir s'en souvenir est considéré indésirable. La bibliothèque tout comme l'écrivain « gémissent, » les deux ayant accumulés trop de « débris » et de « folie, » La description de son mal d'archive en 1965, « le débris incroyable des vieilles lettres en désordre par milliers » rejoint l'image qu'il offre dans *Visions of Cody*, « le désordre incroyable de mon être. » Au bout du compte, et ce malgré sa passion pour l'organisation méthodique, que ce soit dans l'archive, dans l'armoire, ou dans l'âme, Kerouac n'arrive plus à se retrouver. Au moins, aujourd'hui, nous lecteurs chanceux et privilégiés, pouvons le chercher et le retrouver sans problème grâce aux fichiers bien organisés et archivés du catalogue de la bibliothèque la plus proche...ou la plus éloignée.

Notes

[1] En entrevue au *Sel de la semaine* avec Fernand Séguin, à Radio-Canada, le 7 mars 1967, Kerouac se sert du mot *cabane* pour dire *maison*.
[2] 54.1. Jack Kerouac Papers, Henry W. and Albert A. Berg Collection of English and American Literature, New York Public Library. (À partir de maintenant, JKP). Toutes les citations de Kerouac sont tirées des textes en anglais; les traductions sont les miennes.
[3] Jacques Derrida, *Mal de l'archive* (Paris: Galilée, 1995).

Kerouac Corner in the Pollard Memorial Library in Lowell, Massachusetts (courtesy of the Pollard Memorial Library).

Jack Kerouac's Archive Fever

> "I'm grown sick in my papers"
> —Jack Kerouac, *Visions of Gerard*

  Jack Kerouac loved libraries. When he was a boy, in the late 1920s and into the 1930s, he'd read any book lying around in the house and sift through the print matter and ephemera that his father Leo, a local printer in Lowell, Massachusetts, brought back home from the shop. As a teenager he ritualistically played hooky, not (only) to pull a few pranks with his chums around town but also so he could hide away in a secluded corner of the Lowell public library and devour all sorts of books—philosophy, literature, sports, chess strategy, anything—in either French or English. In fact, Kerouac went to the library so often that he eventually established a new record for missing classes at Lowell High School in 1939. Today in the Pollard Library in Lowell you can find a "Kerouac Corner" in honor of the local legend's devotion to reading and books. Kerouac's infatuation with libraries continued during his university studies at Columbia in New York in the early 1940s where he fell in love with the New York Public Library—the same building that today houses the bulk of his archive.¹ In this brief reflection, I suggest that the library is a central site—both figurative and literal—for Kerouac and a crucial context for his overall literary project.

In a 1947 diary, at the age of 25, Kerouac scribbled a short text entitled "On Big City Libraries":

> The two big city libraries that I've had occasion to frequent, the one in Boston and the bigger one in New York, always fill me with an unspeakable feeling of delight when I go to them, a delight that is compounded of these various things: seeing mad old men wander around in deep meditation, seeing pigeons in the court from the window of the library john, seeing pretty girls sitting and reading, and finally participating in a general gloating feeling that this is "culture" of the highest order and that all we who are gathered here are inveterate deep thinkers. I like to stalk around like a mad thinker with my topcoat flying behind me.

"But," Kerouac concluded, "I never have written a decent line in the library" (JKP 54.1). It seems, then, that for this great traveler the library is a site of meditation, of thought, a place where a cultural community of knowledge gathers. Yet this most democratic of institutions is not where he can create his literary oeuvre. That topcoat has to fly, the writing comes "on the run" as he explains in his preface to *Big Sur*—in other words he is a running Proust. And yet, as the extent of the Berg Collection's Jack Kerouac Archive quickly demonstrates, the mad road days were always followed by private months of tedious craftsmanship at his desk, facing his typewriter, surrounded by his filing cabinets brimming with notebooks, letters, newspapers, photographs, and all kinds of ephemera.

Indeed, Kerouac's organizational acumen, the fact that he developed and designed his own original alphanumeric classification system for the majority of his writings, reflects his investment in library science writ large.[2] The library of Kerouac's day, with its file cards and bulky metallic postwar filing cabinets, lies at the foundation of his thought and of his vocational relation to memory, to record-keeping. In the popular imagination, Kerouac is often conjured as a not-so-distant embodiment of some American mystique of the open road and bohemianism, precursor and midwife to the 1960s countercultural revolution. This mediated Kerouac is often (ab)used by critics, many of whom prefer to treat him as some kind of hollow literary piñata that can be whacked in passing as they make their way toward authors whose personal failings they deem less reprehensible than the alcoholic "King of the Beats." After many decades of such easy reification, Kerouac's true literary project largely remains understudied, even invisible, in the United States—with notable exceptions—in part because his archive had not yet been made accessible to the public.[3]

Thankfully, Kerouac is now enjoying a belated and necessary reassessment. While cars and the open road are indeed central to Kerouac's most famous novel, *On the Road,* this focus is part of an ongoing Americanist discourse that has tended to elide for far too long other fundamental sites in Kerouac (not to mention his status as a native French speaker and son of French Canadian immigrants). As I argue in this essay, Kerouac's road narratives are rather centripetal skeins, each one moving or tending toward a center in which the author sits at his desk flanked by his ever-growing archive—what he will later call the "incredible debris." As I hope eventually to show in my current book project, to relocate Kerouac in the archive is to eclipse most critical and popular misconceptions of both his biography and literary contributions to post-World War II American and global literatures. Despite developing a "spontaneous" style, Kerouac is also a revision machine, a careful keeper of records, a cautious comber of details, an "arranger in the manger" with a craving for tracing everything back to its source (*Cody* 29). Douglas Brinkley, the first scholar to be given access to Kerouac's archive in the 1990s—almost a full decade before the Kerouac Papers were opened to researchers in 2006—put it this way: "Kerouac was a fastidious, old-fashioned *craftsman*. For every day he spent 'on the road' during his lifetime, gathering material, he toiled for a month in solitude—sketching, polishing, and typing his various novels, prayers, poems, and reflections" (51). Clark Coolidge offers a more pithy statement: "Kerouac's is not a style. It *is* a practice" ("Jack" 20).

Ann Douglas further judiciously reminds us of the "meticulous and extensive records Kerouac kept of his career and his times; he meant his work to be in some sense verifiable" (12).[4] Verifiability has long been a principal evidentiary function of archives; literary papers reflect not only the labor of a life dedicated to the production of literature, but these proofs of work are also simultaneously proofs of life. Considering the extent of Kerouac's carefully detailed recordkeeping—including countless character charts, event logs, inventories, maps, and diary entries that directly address future readers—Kerouac was not simply seeking the reification of his life and work, but rather hoped that further decryption would one day lead to truer understanding, even for a life as examined as his own. Indeed, even though "Kerouac's life is one of the most chronicled of any twentieth-century author" (Adams 150), his archive continues to yield new texts and new revelations. Thus, although there is much more to unpack in this complex dynamic between Kerouac and the archive, for the purposes of this essay, I offer a concentrated look at his evolving relation to libraries and library technology.

The very idea of libraries, of card catalogues, filing systems, modern record management, provides Kerouac with the shape of his thought and of his relation to memory, and thus to history. In *Visions of Cody*, Kerouac repeatedly offers metatextual reflections on his writing process, namely the excavation of memory *and* of the present moment for literary output. Here is an early example: "the moment is ungraspable, is already gone and if we sleep we can call it up again mixing it with unlimited other beautiful combinations—shuffle the old file cards of the soul in demented hallucinated sleep" (15). With this peculiar turn of phrase, Kerouac suggests that the structure of his own memory is modeled on library technology; for him, the past has taken on the materiality of "file cards" that may now be reshuffled into aesthetically pleasing combinations. As lived moments are "memoried"—Kerouac's verb for a process akin to archiving or, to use a more contemporary analogy, "saving" onto a hard drive—they become remember-able and thus retrievable.[5] They enter Kerouac's card catalogue—what he called his "steeltrap brain,"[6] presumably available for subsequent shuffling. In a way, then, when Kerouac does undertake this shuffling process to extend the Duluoz Legend in written form, he is essentially conducting archival research in the library of his mind. In other words, Kerouac's novelistic method relies on careful record management. Kerouac returns to the "file cards" image later in *Visions of Cody* when he fantasizes about such an organizational system for obtained ideas: "supposing each time you heard a delightfully original idea or were given such an image that makes the mind sing you immediately slapped it over like one of those new office roller files" (49). Ideas and images are filed away in the great rolodex of Kerouac's mind, becoming a dynamic internal archive.

And yet, despite this fantasy and his real-world concern for classification with his own writings, Kerouac was well aware that memory rarely attains such pristine arrangement, and he is haunted by the spectrality of his efforts, the Eros and Thanatos of what Jacques Derrida calls *le mal de l'archive* (archive fever): "I am conscious of my own personal tragedy," Kerouac admits, "my room itself is haunted by it at night when I sleep or wake from a series of restless desperate images, catching myself in the act of shuffling the file cards of the memory or the mind under the deck" (41). Kerouac's greatest fear—tied, crucially, to "the persistent feeling that I'm gonna die soon"—is to be "throwing away something that I can't even find in the incredible clutter of my being but it's going out with the refuse en masse, buried in the middle of it, every now and then I get a glimpse" (41-42). Kerouac thus describes his *mal d'archive,* that trouble, that evil, that insatiable feverish passion that propels him to scour not only the file cards of his memory but also the hidden roads of America. For Derrida, this archive fever means "never to rest, interminably, from searching for the archive right where it slips away. It is to run after the archive, even if there's too much of it, right where something in it anarchives itself" (91). Derrida's impassioned description is thus embodied, with an uncanny resonance, in what Kerouac expresses in *Visions of Cody* when the narrator catches himself "shuffling the file cards of the memory," and realizes that "every now and then I get a glimpse" of that place where it slips away and "anarchives" itself into forgetfulness in "the clutter" of his being (right where "there's too much of it"). The passage helps us understand how Kerouac ended his 47 years of life having accumulated such manuscript mountains, unable to stop himself from digging through that excess clutter, trying to "file" it all away as it ceaselessly expands to form the basis of his novelistic output. It also clarifies his affinity and appreciation for the twentieth-century record-keeping technologies ensconced in those temples of memory we call libraries.

The relation Kerouac entertained with libraries evolved through the years. A few scribbled notes from August 1951—a few months after having typed the *On the Road* scroll—begin with a riff motif of "gray days" and reveal a Kerouac sweetly remembering the childhood "scholarly hours spent in the Lowell HS [High School] library reading the small print of the Encyclopedia Brittanica (1911 edition with the onion skin paper) and later in the Horace Mann library that had ivy outside the windows facing the raw air with the brave certitude of prep school deans, gray days—" (JKP 16.12). It was through these library hours, Kerouac adds, that he "had come to appreciate the Atlantic Seaboard sense of grey days" (JKP 16.12). A month later, while in the midst of one of his most intense periods of physical and psychological identitarian conflict—he was convalescing from a severe attack of thrombophlebitis in the Kingsbridge Veterans Affairs hospital—Kerouac writes in his journal that there is "one thing" he "must always remember in this Canuck dualism crap," namely: "The spirit of *pleasure* in solitary occupations is what I've got to recover from boyhood for manhood's work of art…The huge gray-day preoccupation with files, records, systems, small print, hoary histories in dusty ledgers" (*Unknown* 117). The "gray days" of childhood—which we know from the earlier entry are those spent in libraries—here return not as a source of gloom but rather a source of pleasure, and the basis of his work of art as an adult. Since this insight comes to him while further reflecting on his dual, bilingual identity as both French Canadian and American writer expressing himself mostly in English, it should be stressed that in the wider historical context of Quebec diaspora, such "preoccupation with files, records, systems" was vital to the project of *survivance* which sought to preserve the French Canadian heritage, language, and culture in the midst of the hotbed of assimilation in which Kerouac grew up.[7]

Ultimately, however, Kerouac would lose faith in his archival project. His doubts resurface roughly a year later in August 1952 when he writes: "This is the shortest diary ever kept, tho, because I realize I don't have to keep one—why clutter up the world with my words of daily trivia, etc, it's the sketches and histories and new prose novels that will dump my share of the dirty things into the library bin for the pigs to gobble up" (JKP 15.12). The goal of leaving a "complete record" behind, as he puts it in *Visions of Cody* (99), to "resume commemoration of daily dates, as in hospital promised," no longer seems necessary or destined for the eventual archive ("library bin") (JKP 15.12). Indeed, as the years went by and he accumulated more and more unpublished novels in his rucksack and filing cabinets, Kerouac's archive fever became more and more problematic. In *Visions of Gerard*, composed in 1956, he baldly affirms that the sickness has spread: "I'm grown sick in my papers," a phrase that holds a revealing double temporality, at once present and past tense (*Visions of Cody, Gerard, Big Sur* 545). Despite the fever having reached a new sickening pitch, Kerouac nevertheless went on to undertake his 1965 European trip, as recounted in the last entry to the Duluoz Legend, *Satori in Paris*, with the express goal of finding the genealogical traces of his French and Breton ancestry hidden away in the confines of the great libraries of Paris.

"I was trying to find things out about my old family," he explains in the novella, adding with pride: "I was the first Lebris de Kérouack ever to go back to France in 210 years to find out" (*Satori* 34-35). There is a sense of excitement visible in the early entries of the trip, such as when he writes: "Got the library cased...and am ready for real business Monday" (Diary #47, JKP 58.13). Kerouac even preserved his library card from the National Archives that discloses the seat he occupied on May 30, 1965: No. 329 (Diary #47, JKP 58.13). Alas, as he begins requesting specific material, the "head librarian patiently explains to me that the Nazis done bombed and burned all their French papers in 1944, something which I'd forgotten in my zeal" (*Satori* 22).[8] The library, a site that Kerouac had loved and revered since childhood, has turned into a site of restrictions and ridicule. He ends his first day with an immature lament: "You cant smoke even in the toilet in the Bibliothèque Nationale and you cant get a word in edgewise with the secretaries and there's a national pride about 'scholars' all sitting there copying" (*Satori* 22).

The next day, the archive suddenly grows elusive, and the local authorities seem bent on preventing his access to it. Lost in Paris, Jean-Louis asks directions from a middle-aged *gendarme* (beat cop), but his particular French dialect[9] presents an obstacle to finding—and thus entering—the archive:

> While looking for the library, incidentally, a gendarme in the Place de la Concorde told me that Rue de Richelieu (street of the National Library) was thataway, pointing, and because he was an officer I was afraid to say "What?... NO!" because I knew it was in the opposite direction somewhere—Here he is some kind of sergeant or other who certainly oughta know the streets of Paris giving an American tourist a bum steer. (Or did he believe I was a wise-guy Frenchman pulling his leg? Since my French *is* French). (*Satori* 29-30)

Kerouac's paranoia only amplifies as he speculates that the gendarme was trying to lead him to a spot where they could "shoot down that Québec rat" (*Satori* 30). When he finally makes his way to the Bibliothèque Nationale, the deterioration of his relation to the library intensifies. He suddenly finds himself oppressed by the reading room environment—long gone is that "unspeakable feeling of delight"— the place is now lousy "with thousands of scholars and millions of books and strange assistant librarians with Zen Master brooms (really French aprons) who admire good *handwriting* more than anything in a scholar or writer" (*Satori* 32). Despite appreciating his calligraphy, the librarians are clearly wise to the fact that Mr. Kerouac has been drinking: "Of course," Kerouac self-consciously underscores, "they all smelled the liquor on me and thought I was a nut" (*Satori* 33). When they ask him to leave the premises, Kerouac tellingly defends himself by explaining that he "know[s] libraries!", "and specifically the greatest library in the world, the New York Public Library," and so should not be "regarded with suspicion in the Paris Library" (*Satori* 33). Kerouac's problem, one might say, is that he is, in fact, all too familiar with libraries; he feels so at home in them that he acts in public in a way that is usually only suitable in private.

Later, when his encounters in the French archives prove such a failure, Kerouac not only loses faith in his initial dream to reconnect with his origins, but also in his own lifelong archival project. His final description of the Bibliothèque Nationale stands as a total disavowal:

> The whole library groaned with the accumulated debris of centuries of recorded folly, as tho you had to record folly in the Old or the New World anyhow, like my closet with its incredible debris of cluttered old letters by the thousands, books, dust, magazines, childhood boxscores, the likes of which when I woke up the other night from a pure sleep, made me groan to think this is what I was doing with my waking hours: burdening myself with junk neither I nor anybody else should really want or will ever remember in Heaven. (*Satori* 35)

This passage, culled from the end of the Legend, is a remarkable renunciation of everything Kerouac had once advocated. The history of the world and the private history of a man are here reduced to folly, and the ability to remember is now considered undesirable. Both archive and novelist "groan" with the surfeit of "debris" they have accumulated over the years. The articulation of his *mal d'archive* in 1965 as the "incredible debris of cluttered old letters by the thousands" hauntingly echoes the image of "the incredible clutter of my being" he had offered in *Visions of Cody*.

"Debris," "rubbish," and "junk" had gleefully littered the novelist's earlier, grandiose narratives: in *Visions of Cody* Kerouac had lovingly described "the ordinary city debris of a field" and "the rubbish in the weeds of an empty lot" (70, 40). *Visions of Cody* also describes what was then nothing less than a divine mission to "go groan, go groan alone" (295). But now the groans of man and library seem to express only a "mal d'archive," with Kerouac looking back at his "recorded folly" in dismay; "this is what I was doing with my waking hours?" he sadly asks himself. Now, his painstaking "complete record" seems to have lost its value, haunting him, preventing him from attaining "pure sleep"—that sleep when, in his youth, he used to "shuffle the file cards" of his soul. In the end, and despite his passion for meticulous organization—whether in his files or in his soul—Kerouac could no longer find himself.

Notes

1. Jack Kerouac Papers, Henry W. and Albert A. Berg Collection of English and American Literature, New York Public Library (from now on, JKP). Significant holdings from the *fonds* Kerouac are also housed at Emory University's Stuart A. Rose Manuscript, Archives, and Rare Book Library, Atlanta, GA, and at the Harry Ransom Center, University of Texas at Austin, TX. Smaller collections can also be found elsewhere, such as Columbia University's Rare Book & Manuscript Library.
2. The JKP at the Berg Collection has retained the original order Kerouac had brought to a large portion of his writings. The Series is entitled "Kerouac's arrangement of his archive." See the Jack Kerouac Papers, 1920-1977, Finding Aid: archives.nypl.org/brg/19343#content_structure.
3. I'd also like to underscore the early pioneering studies on Kerouac's oeuvre by Ann Charters, Clark Coolidge, Nancy M. Grace, Tim Hunt, Gerald Nicosia, and Regina Weinreich.
4. See also Ann Charters's groundbreaking essay "Kerouac's Literary Method and Experiments: The Evidence of the Manuscript Notebooks in the Berg Collection," *Bulletin of Research in the Humanities*, vol. 84, no. 4 Winter 1981, pp. 431-50.
5. Variants of "memorying" appear in several moments in *Visions of Cody*, notably on pages 4, 13, and 17.
6. In his *Paris Review* interview, Kerouac says that "a girl once told me that I had a steeltrap brain, meaning I'd catch her with a statement she'd made an hour ago even though our talk had rambled a million lightyears away from that point…" (*Conversations* 70-71).
7. For more on Kerouac, bilingualism, and *survivance*, see Melehy.
8. In his Paris diary, Kerouac does not say that he had "forgotten," but rather that he didn't know: "many of the national records of France were bombed out, which I didn't know" (JKP 58.13).
9. Kerouac grew up in a French Canadian household in New England and did not speak English until he was six years old. The type of French Kerouac spoke—one he often called "patois" or "Canuck," and even "Cajun"—would have been considered heavily accented, even arcane, by European standards. For more on Kerouac's spoken and written French, see Cloutier, "Translator's Note," in *The Unknown Kerouac* (xxiii-xxxiv). See also Melehy; Cloutier, "Avant-Propos: Les Travaux de Jean-Louis Kérouac," in *La vie est d'hommage* (9-48); and Kerouac's letter to Yvonne Le Maître, 8 Sept. 1950, in his *Selected Letters: 1940-1956* (227-229).

Works Cited

Adams, Rachel. *Continental Divides: Remapping the Cultures of North America*. U of Chicago P, 2009.

Brinkley, Douglas. "In the Kerouac Archive." *Atlantic Monthly*, Nov. 1998, pp. 49-77.

Charters, Ann. "Kerouac's Literary Method and Experiments: The Evidence of the Manuscript Notebooks in the Berg Collection." *Bulletin of Research in the Humanities*, vol. 84, no. 4, 1981, pp. 431-50.

Coolidge, Clark. "Jack." Review of *Jack Kerouac: Selected Letters 1940-1956*. *Village Voice*, 11 Apr. 1995, p. 20.

---. *Now It's Jazz: Writings on Kerouac & The Sounds*. Living Batch Press, 1999.

Derrida, Jacques. *Archive Fever: A Freudian Impression*. Translated by Eric Prenowitz, U of Chicago P, 1995.

Douglas, Ann. "'Telepathic shock and meaning excitement': Kerouac's poetics of intimacy." *College Literature*, vol. 27, no. 1, 2000, pp. 8-21.
Jack Kerouac Papers, Henry W. and Albert A. Berg Collection of English and American Literature, New York Public Library, New York, NY.
Kerouac, Jack. *Conversations with Jack Kerouac*. Edited by Kevin J. Hayes, UP of Mississippi, 2005.
---. *Satori in Paris*. Grove Press, 1966.
---. *Selected Letters: 1940-1956*. Edited by Ann Charters, Viking, 1995.
---. *The Unknown Kerouac: Rare, Unpublished, and Newly Translated Writings*. Edited by Todd Tietchen, translated by Jean-Christophe Cloutier, Library of America, 2016.
---. *La vie est d'hommage*. Edited by Jean-Christophe Cloutier, Boréal, 2016.
---. *Visions of Cody*. Penguin, 1972.
---. *Visions of Cody, Visions of Gerard, Big Sur*. Edited by Todd Tietchen, Library of America, 2015.
Melehy, Hassan. *Kerouac: Language, Poetics, & Territory*. Bloomsbury Academic, 2016.

Virus and Word Virus: David Wojnarowicz, HIV/AIDS, and The Beat Generation
Jonathan Sedberry

Though some readers reduce the Beat writers to promiscuous hedonists who, at best, produced entertaining works that countered the lock-step conformity of the 1950s and, at worst, appropriated for profit and fame others' cultures, the well-documented contributions of Jack Kerouac as a pop-culture shaman and prolific writer and of Allen Ginsberg as a literary benefactor and cultural paragon, particularly for the hippie movement, provide a platform to attend to the sociopolitical and aesthetic legacy of the Beat writers. This includes the enigmatic William S. Burroughs whose opaque style, taboo-cum-recondite subjects, and discommoding biography often cause even bibliomaniacs to know him only as the man who wrote *a* novel (*Naked Lunch* 1958) and people with particular cultural taste (and often of a certain age) to know him as the random older gentleman in *Drugstore Cowboy* and a Nike commercial, to (unknowingly) experience his words and voice through his collaborations with Kurt Cobain and Tom Waits, and to (unwittingly) reference him when discussing Steely Dan. Burroughs's cultural import extends beyond a single novel and miscellany of cultural one-offs, as he influenced writers in the generations that followed the publication of *Junkie* (1953). Not all of these writers joined David Foster Wallace in seeing an enemy: "'If I have an enemy,' he said in the early 1990s, 'a patriarch for my patricide, it's probably Barth and Coover and Burroughs, even Nabokov and Pynchon'" (Scott). Burroughs's devotion to revealing mechanisms of control inspired mixed-media artist David Wojnarowicz, while Burroughs's worldview and Kerouac's writing style provided Wojnarowicz a vehicle for addressing the HIV/AIDS epidemic. Though born too late (1954) for association with the Beat generation at its collective zenith, Wojnarowicz shares much with that group, for his art, particularly chapter six of *Close to the Knives: A Memoir of Disintegration* (1991), survives as an extension of the aesthetic and sociopolitical insurgence the Beats writers pursued, so examining Wojnarowicz through the lens of the Beat movement, especially through Burroughs and Kerouac, provides readers insight into the lasting impact of the Beat writers while increasing the visibility of a marginalized HIV/AIDS canon. Wojnarowicz writes that he

> saw his boyhood home of Red Bank, New Jersey as a tiny version of hell called the suburbs [where he] experienced the Universe of the Neatly Clipped Lawn. This is a place where anything and everything can and does take place—and events such as torture, starvation, humiliation, physical and psychotic violence can take place uncontested by others, as long as it doesn't stray across boundaries and borders as formed by the deed-holder inhabiting

the house on the neatly clipped lawn. If the violence is contained within the borders of the lawn and does not mess up the real estate in any way that would cause the surrounding properties devaluation, anything is possible and everything permissible [sic]. (*Close* 151)

Through language that recalls Burroughs's use of Hassan-i-Sabbah, Wojnarowicz understates his suburban experience, for after his parents divorced when he was two, he and his two sisters lived with his indifferent, affectionless mother until his violent, alcoholic father kidnapped him and his siblings only to abuse them—sexually, physically, and psychologically—and return them when his interest waned. Journalist Richard Woodward notes how having also spent some time in an orphanage, Wojnarowicz "seems to have spent much of his adolescence in agony that his homosexuality and his dysfunctional family did not square with the ideals of the 50's" (H1), the same ideals Burroughs was subverting as a response, in part, to his childhood agony, wrought from his sexuality.

Wojnarowicz turned to sex work at age nine, and by 13 he explored his complex, guilt-laden sexual appetite through frequent sex work and random encounters, often with married men whom he picked up in the pornographic theaters of Times Square. In addition to his body, Wojnarowicz sold pornographic sketches to his friends. With these sketches, he developed his talent, eventually earning entry into New York's High School of Music and Art, though he dropped out at sixteen. In the early 1970s, Wojnarowicz tried writing poetry as an extension of his art and obsessed over the works of Rimbaud, Genet, and Kerouac, whose *Tristessa* Wojnarowicz sought out even when living as a vagabond. Biographer Cynthia Carr remarks that Wojnarowicz "romanticized [Kerouac's] life" on the road and saw "it as a model for how to think about his own experience" (55). Wojnarowicz roamed around the Mid-Atlantic states, eventually embarking on a round-trip, cross-country hitchhike in 1976.

By 1976, he had discovered the work of Burroughs; Wojnarowicz's former roommate, Peeka Trenkle, recalls how "'he was enamored of William Burroughs and Jack Kerouac and this sort of self-destructive brilliance—he loved that and we used to have talks about it'" (qtd. in Carr 61). Before and during this cross-country trek, Wojnarowicz wrote less poetry, choosing to collect journal stories he called monologues, which became his first book, *Sounds in the Distance* (1982, later reissued in 1996 as *The Waterfront Journals*). Burroughs wrote the forward for this collection after mutual friend Herbert Huncke connected the two men. Wojnarowicz befriended Huncke after a chance encounter at a laundromat with Louis Cartwright who lived with Huncke, the originator of the term *beat*. Huncke became the object of desire and a role model for Wojnarowicz, who, having spent his teens as a hustler, delinquent, sex worker, and thief, had biographical points of contact with Huncke.

As the 1970s progressed, Wojnarowicz continued to read Burroughs and Kerouac, adding the poetry of Lawrence Ferlinghetti and the poetry and lyrics of Patti Smith, who, like Huncke, kept Wojnarowicz connected to Burroughs. Through these connections, he developed a stronger attraction to Burroughs than to Kerouac, though his interest was in the amalgam of Burroughs the man and Burroughs the myth. As he wrote in *In the Shadow*,

> I realize that my attraction to Burroughs is based on a great deal of his personal mystique, that which has been built up around him by biography and accounts of Burroughsian madness in old letters and magazines and descriptions and the culminating sense of wild head drug stuff that I get off on for the satisfaction of knowing and learning of scenes that connect with maybe unexplored desired areas of sociological truth that are clearly spoken in some of his books. (74-75)

The attraction to this "mystique" inspired Wojnarowicz to attempt to transform Burroughs's *The Wild Boys* into a film and was one catalyst leading Wojnarowicz to collage. In 1979, he "completed the first collage that would remain part of his oeuvre, *Bill Burroughs' Recurring Dream*—using a photo of Burroughs bought in a Left Bank shop and an image of a centipede bought from a Seine stall" (Carr 122). He continued to compose journal entries, but more and more, his public writing was included as a component of his photography, paintings, and collages.

By the 1980s, Wojnarowicz's art was replete with frank, graphic homoeroticism. Social and political conservatives condemned his art, which included the photographic collage *Fuck You Faggot Fucker* (1984),[1] because they deemed it vulgar and disturbing, just as they had Beat productions in the 1950s, and as with Beat writers, a diverse collection of individuals[2] championed Wojnarowicz for dedicating his career to honoring outsiders, blending the public and private spheres, and combating hatred, stigmatization, and homophobia. His art became more radical and angrier after he was diagnosed as HIV-positive (1988) and until his death (1992) of AIDS-related infection. As the end of his life neared, he again turned to writing as an artistic form often distinct from his other art. During this period, he composed the texts that became *Close to the Knives*.

In drafting the pieces that became his memoir, Wojnarowicz, like Burroughs, recognized the limitations of language while paradoxically noting how language exists as a powerful mechanism through which to control people and culture. He utilized a method, akin to Kerouac's spontaneous prose, to offer what Burroughs was unable or unwilling to provide: an unfiltered depiction of the effects of HIV/AIDS and outspoken criticism of the rhetoricians condemning gay men.

Burroughs was a gay man whose fiction belongs (not solely) to the queer canon because of its influence on subsequent queer artists, yet the obituarists who addressed his life merely mention his sexuality while focusing on his drug addiction, uxoricide, WASP bohemianism, and writing, though from the 1950s through the first decade of the twenty-first century, critics offered heterocentric readings that align him with the canon of the avant-garde and that note his sexuality as part of the cultural rebellion the Beat writers pursued instead of as an inspiration, especially for the pre-Stonewall LGBTQ community. In *Queer Burroughs*, Jamie Russell outlines how "the American literary tradition has...managed to overlook, ignore, or shun Burroughs' queer status" (3). After assessing this neglect, Russell takes Burroughs to task for employing sexual passing to mask gay sexuality and for choosing to evade explicit recognition of the HIV/AIDS epidemic and the havoc it wrought in the American gay community of the 1980s and 1990s, correctly claiming that any attention to the latter was incidental. Russell explains how "the extent of Burroughs' silence about the issue is particularly surprising given his fascination with viruses and disease and his membership in two of the communities most at risk from the virus (as gay man and former junkie)" (161). However, decades spent employing art to fight social repression allowed Burroughs to contribute to the HIV/AIDS canon through his connection with Wojnarowicz, whose career countered the hateful rhetoric coloring the first decade of the epidemic.

As with Burroughs's attention to addicts, Wojnarowicz represented an underclass: HIV-positive homeless who embody facets of the amalgam of his identity—hustlers, criminals, sex workers. Whereas the heterocentric media proffered images of the innocent, Ryan White-like victims of HIV and the gay press sanitized the truth with photos of white, middle-class gay men, Wojnarowicz represented the homeless, destitute street hustler, whose presence no one wanted to acknowledge; the uninsurable sex worker who family, culture, and society victimized; and in his most memorable work,[3] himself, the agonized misfit cast aside by family and left behind by friends dead from HIV-related opportunistic infections. His diagnosis allowed him to find the freedom of expression he began looking for in his adolescent sketches: "at the moment of diagnosis I fully gave up that desire to fit in and started realizing that those places where I didn't fit and the ways I was diverse were the most interesting parts of myself" (qtd. in Woodward H1). In defense of the underclasses, he challenged the medical community and the federal government for their complicity with death. He also took aim at the media and the unaffected community, exemplified by the following passage from *Close*:

> I hear endless news stories of murder around the nation where the defendant claims self-defense because this queer tried to touch him and the defendant being freed and I'm lying here on this bed of Peter's[4] that was the scene of an intense illness and the channel of the tv has been turned to some show about the cost of AIDS and I'm watching a group of people die on camera because they can't afford the drugs that might extend their lives and some fella in the healthcare system in texas is being interviewed—I can't even remember what he looks like because I reached through the television screen and ripped his face in half—he's saying, "If I had a dollar to spend for health care I'd rather spend it on a baby or an innocent person with some illness or defect not of their own responsibility; not some person with AIDS." (105)

Encounters with homophobia and with those who refused to see him as a human, and HIV as a universal threat to humanity, spurred his activism, which infiltrated his art. In constructing his post-diagnosis movement, he determined that with his writing he was "not so much interested in creating literature as [he was] in trying to convey the pressure of what [he had] witnessed or experienced" (*In the Shadow* 235). With a style recalling the free-flowing compositions of Kerouac and the rule-defying syntax of Burroughs, Wojnarowicz lays bare his love for Peter, reminds his audience that sexuality includes love, and begins to release his anger. Craft was less important to him than content. Instead of agonizing over the perfect metaphor, he recorded his raw emotion and visceral reaction.

From his early monologues to his memoir, Wojnarowicz's writing does not fit neatly into such traditional genres as fiction, journalism, or personal narrative. Rather, it reads as a hybrid that combines aspects of traditional forms—a collage of styles drawing upon whatever aesthetic serves the moment—with revealing, inventive forms of his own creation. Of his mordant autobiographical writings, the collected texts of *Close* stand, because of the style, attitude, and energy, as a testament to the Beat generation and as a profound microcosm of his artistic agenda and sensibility, which shaped a counter-rhetoric that freed him from the restraints of traditional formal writing.

Though certain parallels exist between what Michel Foucault identifies as *counter-discourse* and what I am calling *counter-rhetoric*, counter-rhetoric does not develop only from the formerly voiceless who appropriate discourses of oppression to counter the prevailing authoritative discourses. I propose *counter-rhetoric* as the term for the rhetoric of response, open to anyone who wishes to challenge a previously articulated idea, theory, characterization, or doctrine developed through traditional forms of rhetoric. I intend *counter-rhetoric* to identify the artistic and political imperatives driving the composition of *Close*.

Rhetoric is "the art of using language so as to persuade or influence others" (*OED*). Jessie Helms, William Dannemeyer, and other public figures employed rhetoric to persuade the general population to think of HIV/AIDS as a necessary punishment for hedonistic, immoral actions. Wojnarowicz counters their rhetoric with his own, which he intends to have the opposite effect: to educate through brutally honest, colloquial, often vulgar rhetoric. In this context, *counter-rhetoric* indicates a retort to the artful rhetoric of the heteronormative cultural agenda—a rejoinder that contradicts odious misinformation; offers statistics that counteract rumor, innuendo, and exaggeration; and honors the bravery of the underclasses. *Counter-rhetoric* thus also stands for an alternative style to the eloquent writing of conservative rhetoricians. An anonymous reviewer describes the collection as "written in a free-form, onrushing style [that] might be compared to Beat prose with an apocalyptic hue" ("On the Knife-edge"). Aside from the reviewer's failure to understand how an apocalyptic hue often shadows Beat prose, especially in the work of Burroughs, this observer correctly testifies to the essence of this denotation of *counter-rhetoric*. In the final instance, I intend *counter-rhetoric* to stand for the question of whether the "faculty of using eloquent or persuasive language" (*OED*) can function in the environment of HIV/AIDS—of whether language can express the virus and its effects. In the context of these questions, Wojnarowicz's usage of counter-rhetoric questions the very nature of language as a communicative force—a question Burroughs posed as well.

Of the texts included in *Close*, "Postcards from America"—in particular, the portion "X-Rays from Hell"—stands out not only for its counter-attention to HIV/AIDS and its sensitivity towards the suffering of others, but for its controversy. With "Postcards from America," the title suggests how Wojnarowicz understands the form of the three separate texts contained therein: snippets of experience, images from foreign places. People often send postcards to share the image captured on the card or to relay a message from a trip away from home and an image that represents that trip. The three texts of "Postcards from America"—"X-Rays from Hell," "The Seven Deadly Sins Fact Sheet," and "Additional Statistics and Facts"—each communicate ideas and images Wojnarowicz encounters from his literal and imaginative trips to "foreign" places: the streets, the shadows, the outskirts of America, the imagination, and the truth, a space made foreign by the heteronormative cultural agenda's equivocal depictions of the epidemic. Wojnarowicz offers three distinct forms of written postcards that allow him to introduce his visual emphasis in his essay. Though "X-Rays from Hell" is the most intriguing and developed of the three sections, the other two capture important details through inventive rhetorical forms.

The second piece in "Postcards from America"—"The Seven Deadly Sins Fact Sheet"—offers a systematic critique of seven individuals Wojnarowicz identifies as responsible for the spread of AIDS, including the aforementioned Cardinal John O'Connor, Representative William E. Dannemeyer, and Senator Jesse Helms as well as New York City Mayor Edward Koch, New York City Health Commissioner Stephen Joseph, New York Senator Alfonse D'Amato, and Frank Young, the head of the Food and Drug Administration. *Fact-sheet* denotes "a paper on which facts relevant to a particular issue are set out briefly and clearly" (*OED*). Wojnarowicz manipulates this form, turning a fact-sheet into a rhetorical form that operates as a variety of his expository postcard, as he includes snippets of pertinent information. Ignoring grammar, Wojnarowicz spews enraged charges against the "seven deadly sins." For example, he argues that "Koch has stalled, ranted, and raved, and in general done everything he could to avoid dealing with the AIDS crisis" (*Close* 124). The "everything" includes turning his back on the "8,000-10,000 P.W.A.'s[5]...homeless in the streets" (*Close* 124). Wojnarowicz demonstrates his acute sensitivity by drawing attention to the conditions of the homeless—here with anger directed toward the mayor, whereas in "X-Rays from Hell" he responds with empathy for the homeless. He does offer one compliment to one of the sins, for he notes how "under Helms, words and pictures have gained a power they haven't had in decades compared to television" (*Close* 129)—a beneficial change for Wojnarowicz's counter-rhetoric.

The third text in "Postcards from America," "Additional Statistics and Facts," articulates important data related to the epidemic and counters the misconceptions developed and perpetuated by mainstream and/or conservative rhetoric about the epidemic, including the press's notion that Wojnarowicz's anger springs not from actual injustice but from personal anguish from having contracted HIV. He admonishes the press for such an observation, pointing out that, first, "anybody has the right to be outraged and the right to express these things," and, second, he had been "writing about these issues in this [angry] 'tone' well before [his] diagnosis with AIDS" (*Close* 136). This postcard serves as another version of the fact-sheet. In this version, he focuses less on who is to blame for the epidemic and more on what he feels people should know. Instead, he blames those who withhold the information he has discovered and wishes to disseminate.

Reading like extended versions of the explanatory blurbs on the backs of picture postcards, "The Seven Deadly Sins Fact Sheet" and "Additional Statistics and Facts" express Wojnarowicz's anger, which develops from "feeling all this outside pressure that demands that [he] feel guilty or afraid" (Interview with Goldin 61). He intends these two pieces to demonstrate how "now is not the time for restraint to be shown in the form of our words and gestures, for men like Helms, Dannemeyer, or O'Connor show little restraint in their zeal to trample the Constitution" (*Close* 137). He responds to mainstream and conservative rhetoric with unrefined but effective counter-rhetoric. Though the facts and rage these sections offer fulfill his intention, they fail to match the magisterial tone, impassioned sensitivity, vigorous style, and controversial notions in "X-Rays from Hell."

Wojnarowicz first included "X-Rays from Hell" in the show "WITNESS: Against Our Vanishing," which the Manhattan gallery Artists Space hosted. The National Endowment for the Arts withdrew its grant because of the piece, though their gesture was years in the making. Most of the controversy stems from Wojnarowicz's identification of Cardinal O'Connor as the "fat cannibal from that house of walking swastikas" (*Close* 114), as well as from his celebration of the imagination, which Wojnarowicz identified as "one of the last frontiers left for radical gesture"—a space in which he can fantasize "dous[ing] Helms with a bucket of gasoline" or "throw[ing] congressman William Dannemeyer off the empire state building" (*Close* 120). What gets lost when an audience focuses on these images and the language that builds them is the power of Wojnarowicz's counter-rhetoric and the intricacy of his style.

Though regularly transmitting odious, hateful observations, various examples of HIV/AIDS-related rhetoric often emanate from structured, traditional, eloquent prose and from articulate, expressive oratory. But even ardent fans would struggle to characterize Wojnarowicz's style as such. In "X-Rays from Hell," he marries the energy, unruliness, and loquacity of Hunter S. Thompson's Gonzo journalism[6] to the posture, ethics, decadence, and street speak of protopunker Iggy Pop, the countercultural icon from whom Wojnarowicz procures one of his epigraphs. Moreover, in *Close to the Knives*, the scope and direction of style resembles spontaneous prose as defined by Kerouac because instead of order or "'selectivity' of expression," the style follows "free deviation (association) of mind into limitless blow-on-subject seas of thought, swimming in sea of English with no discipline other than rhythms of rhetorical exhalation and expostulated statement, like a fist coming down on a table with each complete utterance, bang!" (Kerouac, "Essentials" 484). For example, in "Self-Portrait in Twenty-Three Rounds," the essay that opens *Close*, Wojnarowicz begins with a meditation on his heritage tracking to "some faraway sun-filled bed" before turning, two sentences later, to the memory of a night spent at a drag queen's house:

> My buddy knocked on the door to try and get a mattress to lay down on she sent a bullet through the door thinking it was her man—after three days of no sleep and maybe a couple of stolen donuts my eyes start separating: one goes left and one goes right and after four days of sitting on some stoop on a side street head cradled in my arms seeing four hours of pairs of legs walking by too much traffic noise and junkies trying to rip us off and the sunlight so hot this is a new york summer I feel my brains slowly coming to a boil in whatever red-blue liquid the brains float in and looking down the street or walking around I begin to see large rats the size of shoeboxes. (4)

The portrait continues in this fashion, without regard to grammar but with regard to visual language. Wojnarowicz is one of Kerouac's "mad ones" and his style, his "free deviation (association) of mind," reflects his energy, as he cannot contain his expression within properly punctuated sentences.

Despite this free, shifting style, Wojnarowicz's written voice, as in all "his work, in all media is clear, singular, monumental," claims critic Elizabeth Hess (33). As when poet Paul Monette fired his verbal, poetic Uzi,[7] "when David screamed," his audience "listened and the enemy shuddered" (Hess 33). The structure of "X-Rays from Hell," with Wojnarowicz's deviation from the supposed conversation with a fellow PWA, allows him to explore a number of topics roughly associated with his friend's "agitating FEAR" (*Close* 111). The structure of this expository postcard allows Wojnarowicz to wander through a myriad of topics associated with fear and to weave together his artistic observations of life on the outside with his denunciations of the heteronormative establishment. His style aligns with what he learned reading Kerouac: the best writing stems from "the most painful personal wrung-out tossed from the cradle warm protective mind" (Kerouac, "Essentials" 485). This style challenges the role of formal rhetoric in an epidemic, calling into question the distance formal rhetoric affords the rhetorician, the nature of craft, and the appropriateness of eloquent language and style, whether in support or in condemnation of PWAs. In some passages, Wojnarowicz's writing also approaches Burroughs's cut-up, as he includes real conversations as if they were pure invention, but he found more inspiration in Burroughs's worldview and philosophy of language than in his style.

"X-Rays from Hell" begins with Wojnarowicz cutting in a real experience as an imagined recollection of a previous afternoon when "a friend came over unexpectedly to sit at [Wojnarowicz's] kitchen table and try to find some measure of language for his state of mind" (*Close* 111). Finding a "measure of language" with which to consider, address, and discuss HIV/AIDS has been the goal of nearly every writer, critic, and theorist confronting the epidemic as subject. After several pages in which he digresses into a myriad of topics (exploring Kerouac's ideal), Wojnarowicz returns to language:

> I am busying myself with a process of distancing myself from you and others and my environment in order to know what I feel and what I can find. I'm trying to lift off the weight of the preinvented world so I can see what's underneath it all. I'm hungry and the preinvented world won't satisfy my hunger. I'm a prisoner of language that doesn't have a letter or a sign or gesture that approximates what I'm sensing. Rage may be one of the few things that binds or connects me to you, to our preinvented world. (*Close* 116-17)

In a letter to his first wife, Edie Kerouac-Parker, Kerouac wrote a free-verse poem in which he claims, "The world you see is just a movie in your mind" (*Selected Letters* 7). Like Burroughs, Wojnarowicz thought the movie was predetermined and projected into the mind. He did not want to follow the script of the preinvented world. Language is a part of what constructs the preinvented world that ostracizes the underclasses whom Wojnarowicz and Burroughs honored. They sought to manipulate language in order to shatter this construction of reality, to "deafen the satellites and lift the curtains surrounding the control room," as he writes in *Close* (123).

Familiar with the rhetoric of AIDS, Wojnarowicz cannot escape the entanglements of such rhetoric nor can he locate the proper word for what he is sensing. Given the parameters of modern society, his inability to find the necessary word results in an inability to communicate outwardly his private sensation. He has come to believe no such word exists. Through this absence, language imprisons him, so he realizes why Burroughs described language as a virus—a talk sickness—and why Burroughs revised the opening verse of John to "In the beginning was the word and the word was bullshit. The beginning words came out on the con clawing for traction" (*The Ticket* 198). Words "c[o]me out on the con" because they trick the user into thinking they are more than just depthless signifiers and that a word exists to communicate every experience.

To discover what he truly feels, Wojnarowicz must escape language, but the task eludes him because the languages of hate, prejudice, symptomatology, virology, culture, and various other fields color his mind. This presence and influence of language prompted Burroughs to define language as a virus from which people cannot escape:

> The "Other Half" is the word. The "Other Half" is an organism. Word is an organism [...] From symbiosis to parasitism is a short step. The word is now a virus. The flu virus may once have been a healthy lung cell. It is now a parasitic organism that invades and damages the lungs. The word may have once been a healthy neural cell. It is now a parasitic organism that invades and damages the central nervous system. Modern man has lost the option of silence. Try halting your sub-vocal speech. Try to achieve even ten seconds of inner silence. You will encounter a resisting organism that *forces you to talk*. That organism is the word. (*The Ticket* 49)

As a result of the politics and rhetoric of AIDS, Wojnarowicz, like Burroughs, understands how language controls individuals, how words "are made to lie with" (Burroughs, *Last Words* 38), and how language and its users produce a construct of the world: "word begets image and image is virus" (Burroughs, *Nova Express* 48). This construct into which everyone is born—the "preinvented world" for Wojnarowicz, the Reality Studio for Burroughs—controls through language. Like Burroughs, Wojnarowicz decided that if he could not escape language, he would turn the weapon against itself and against his enemies to spark others to activism. These ideas of language and reality combine with Wojnarowicz's style to counter the eloquent rhetoric of conservatives, though he does not counter their rhetoric with only abstractions and style. He targets Helms, O'Connor, the respected arts community, and others, but the outstanding invectives in "X-Rays from Hell" include his selfless observation of the homeless and poor and his critique of the "ONE-TRIBE NATION" (*Close* 121): "We are born into a pre invented existence within a tribal nation of zombies and in that illusion of a one-tribe nation there are real tribes" (*Close* 37). *ONE-TRIBE NATION* is the ironic signifier critiquing the sameness the Beat movement sought to subvert. This sameness is a construct the media propagates: "The generic upper and upper middle-class group information/illusion fed us X number of hours a day. The information applies to a mythic 'general public' and that is used by politicians and fundamentalists and anyone trying to set a particular structure in place and have it enforced morally or otherwise by institutions" (Wojnarowicz interview, "Idol Worship" 464). Art can reveal the real tribes living under the broadcast singularity.

The life conditions of the poor, homeless, and drug-addicted magnify any HIV/AIDS-related issue, yet few of the unaffected and/or uninfected care. Having subsisted for significant portions of his life amongst these individuals, Wojnarowicz cannot accept others' denial of the plight of such outcasts. His activist rhetoric written on their behalf not only runs counter to the conservative social rhetoric but to the activist rhetoric itself. He does not just call for practical, short-term solutions, such as needle exchange programs; he demands empathy just as he demands outrage and radical gestures. If fulfilled, these ultimatums will aid in the attack against the ONE-TRIBE NATION, which Wojnarowicz sought to expose even before his diagnosis.

Exposure creates the possibility for "an X-ray of Civilization, an examination of its foundations" (*Close* 121). The foundations reveal the "millions of tribes" hidden by the government's illusion of the one tribe (*Close* 121). An x-ray exposes what lays beneath, hence the title of this postcard: "X-Rays from Hell." The stigmatization surrounding HIV/AIDS has created the possibility for a living hell, as has the disease itself and the medication (AZT)[8] for "treating" it. In this postcard, Wojnarowicz seeks to expose the lie of the preinvented world, to reveal obscured facts about the epidemic and the nation, and to provide an image of the individuals lost in the perpetuation of the notion of the "general public." In his visual work, Wojnarowicz often combined collage, photographic double exposure, shadowing, and other manipulative techniques to give his images the appearance of an x-ray. For example, in the "Sex Series" (1988-1989), Wojnarowicz offers large images—of cities, forests, and other common places—to which he attaches gay pornographic images that he encircles to set them apart from the larger image but also to give the appearance of something magnified, something exposed. The series suggests what takes place behind the common images, behind the lie of the one-tribe nation. In "X-Rays from Hell," Wojnarowicz applies his sensibility as a visual artist to expose what lies behind the myths of the heteronormative cultural agenda propagated as well as the lies and misinformation inherent in mainstream and conservative rhetoric. He wants to show the projector of the Reality Studio.

In "Essentials of Spontaneous Prose," Kerouac orders writers to look to the muse within because their way is the only true away, "always honest, ('ludicrous'), spontaneous, 'confessional,' interesting, because not 'crafted.' Craft *is* craft" (485). Wojnarowicz's multi-function counter-rhetoric, with its bounding digressions and syntactic escapades, follows Kerouac's orders, offering a polymorphous discourse on the HIV/AIDS epidemic, politics, language, reality, and "A DISEASED SOCIETY AS WELL" (*Close* 114). Wojnarowicz's activist counter-rhetoric developed from his outsiderness, his desire "to leave a record" so that "some of [his] experience [lives] on" (Interview with Goldin 62), and his desire to let others know they are not as alone as they may think. According to Vince Passaro, it is because of this desire that "in the downtown literary milieu, which gained its energy in a fluctuating pattern of angry posturing and caustic irony, Wojnarowicz stands somewhat apart: he is more tolerant, more witty, full of anger and violence but anger and violence surrounded by a halo of calm and an eerie sense of beauty." David Breslin, Penny Kaganoff, Michael Martin, and other critics have compared him to Kerouac and Jean Genet because like them, he speaks, through his art, for a sector of society alienated and silenced by institutions, manners, government, and death, while his attention to exposure connects him to Burroughs. *Close to the Knives* witnesses the suffering HIV/AIDS caused American underclasses in the 1980s, but it also testifies to the Beat movement's lasting sphere of influence.

Notes

[1] The background of the collage presents a map of the world with the nations shredded, cut, and spread throughout the oceans. Centered in the foreground, two men kiss with bodies partially turned toward each other, each with one arm embracing the other man, and one arm, bent suggestively at the elbow, immersed in the water. They stand bare and waist-deep in water, with the partial map of North America superimposed on their bodies. In the northeast, northwest, and southwest corners of the collage, Wojnarowicz includes the same photo of two naked men—one sitting, one standing—both of whom stare out at the audience. In the southeast corner, a lone, shirtless man stands with three cupid-esque arrows lodged in him and three, shadowy, small fighter jets circling behind him. Below the image of the two men kissing is a clipping of a school-age-type doodle of one man having anal intercourse with another. The man in front carries the labels "faggot" and "oo la la," while the man behind, the man who is penetrating the other, carries the label "faggot fucker," above which is written "FUCK YOU." Following the illogical logic of hatred, the labels suggest that a "faggot" can be insulted and dismissed (with the torn, additional label "eats shit"), but a "faggot fucker" deserves additional hatred and derision.
[2] Champions include Fran Lebowitz, Jonathan David Katz, and William S. Burroughs.
[3] *Close to the Knives*, various mixed-media self-portraits, and the Rimbaud series, which includes photographs of Wojnarowicz, in various poses, wearing a paper mask of Rimbaud's face.
[4] Photographer Peter Hujar was Wojnarowicz's life partner until he died in 1987 from AIDS-related pneumonia.
[5] Person/People with AIDS.
[6] Though perhaps not his intention, Thompson developed a preeminent form of activist writing because it combines the first two, previously separated, activist writer's activities (actions first, experience second) and allows the third step (reflection) to become part of the initial process of reporting. Through a marriage of committed, subjective journalism and factual distortion as reported through exaggerated rhetorical style, Gonzo journalism as used by subsequent writers serves as an apt response to the social milieu of AIDS.
[7] In the Preface to his *Love Alone: 18 Elegies for Rog*, Paul Monette recalls how he approached craft when facing an epidemic desecrating his community and killing his partner, Roger Horwitz: "When I began to write about AIDS during Roger's illness, I wanted a form that would move with breathless speed, so I could scream if I wanted and rattle on and empty my Uzi into the air" (xii).
[8] Azidothymidine, also called zidovudine, was approved in 1987 as the first drug to prolong the life of PWAs.

Works Cited

Burroughs, William S. *Last Words: The Final Journals of William S. Burroughs*. Edited by James Grauerholz, Grove Press, 2000.
---. *Nova Express*. 1964. Grove Press, 1992.
---. *The Ticket That Exploded*. 1962. Grove Press, 1967.
Carr, Cynthia. *Fire in the Belly: The Life and Times of David Wojnarowicz*. Bloomsbury, 2012.
"Fact." Def. 8. *Oxford English Dictionary*.

Hess, Elizabeth. Untitled essay. *David Wojnarowicz: Brush Fires in the Social Landscape*. Edited by Melissa Harris, Aperture Foundation, 1994, pp. 32-33.

Kerouac, Jack. "The Essentials of Spontaneous Prose." 1953. *The Portable Jack Kerouac*. Edited by Ann Charters, Penguin, 1995, pp. 484-85.

---. *Selected Letters, 1957-1969*. Edited by Ann Charters, Penguin, 1999.

Monette, Paul. Preface. *Love Alone: 18 Elegies for Rog*. St. Martin's Press, 1988.

"On the Knife-edge with Wojnarowicz and Vintage." *Publishers Weekly* 1 Feb. 1991, *InfoTrac*.

Passaro, Vince. "The Last Outsider." *Bookends*, 12 Mar. 2000, *NYTimes.com*, archive.www.nytimes.com/www.nytimes.com/books/00/03/12/bookend/bookend.html. Accessed 24 Aug. 2018.

"Rhetoric." Def. 1.a., 2.a., and 3. *Oxford English Dictionary*.

Russell, Jamie. *Queer Burroughs*. Palgrave, 2001.

Scott, A.O. "The Best Mind of His Generation." *The New York Times*, 20 Sept. 2008, www.nytimes.com/2008/09/21/weekinreview/21scott.html. Accessed 25 July 2018.

Wojnarowicz, David. *Close to the Knives: A Memoir of Disintegration*. 1991. Serpent's Tail, 1992.

---. "Idol Worship: Talking with David Wojnarowicz." Interview with Owen Keehnen. Aug 1991. *We're Here, We're Queer...in Short: The Gay 90's and Beyond*. Prairie Avenue Productions, 2011, pp. 461-67.

---. *In The Shadow of the American Dream: The Diaries of David Wojnarowicz*. Edited by May Scholder, Grove Press, 1999.

---. Interview with Nan Goldin. 1991. *David Wojnarowicz: Brush Fires in the Social Landscape*. Edited by Melissa Harris, Aperture Foundation, 1994, pp. 57-62.

Woodward, Richard B. "All the Rage, Posthumously." *New York Times*, 7 May 1995, H1.

The Beat Interview
Bobbie Louise Hawkins

Courtesy of Naropa University Archive, n.d., photographer unknown.

Home Movies by Bobbie Louise Hawkins
Ronna C. Johnson and Nancy M. Grace

The *Journal of Beat Studies* Interview this year is a consolidation of two interviews with writer Bobbie Louise Hawkins, conducted at her home in Boulder, Colorado, by Ronna C. Johnson and Nancy M. Grace in 2001 and 2002. A consummate storyteller, Hawkins tells a life story filled with grit and humor, as she moved from being a Baptist preacher at the age of 12 in Texas to visual artist studying with Lucian Freud in London to actor to writer to performer to educator.

Hawkins died on May 4, 2018, in Boulder, Colorado, and was born on July 11, 1930, in Abilene, Texas, the only child of her young mother, who raised her with her stepfather and extended family; when Hawkins was in fifth grade, they moved to Albuquerque, New Mexico. From there, after graduating from high school at age 15, Hawkins left the U.S. Southwest for Denmark, London, British Honduras (now Belize), Japan, and back to New Mexico for a time; then onward into the productive art and literary scenes of Bolinas, California, and Boulder.

A prolific writer and a long-time faculty member of the Jack Kerouac School for Disembodied Poetics at Naropa University, Hawkins over the years generously shared her life stories with scholars and students alike. In this distillation of some of those stories, she comments on her early days as a child preacher in a Baptist church, initial training as a painter—studying with Freud at the Slade School of Fine Art of the University College London—marriage and divorce to Danish architect Olaf Hoeck (1949-1956), subsequent 18-year marriage and then divorce from poet Robert Creeley (1957-1976), her international and domestic travels, her writing practices, and her candid commentary on Beat and Beat-movement associated writers including Joanne Kyger, Diane di Prima, Anne Waldman, Allen Ginsberg, and Lew Welch.

Of particular note are her memories of her struggles to write two of her novels, *One Small Saga* (Coffee House Press, 1985) and *The Sanguine Breast of Margaret* (North and South Press, 1992). She makes clear that she considered herself a prose writer foremost and then a poet, one nurtured in the heady company of mid-twentieth-century American literary communities featuring Charles Olson, di Prima, Robert Duncan, Jess Collins, Denise Levertov, Michael and Joanna McClure, Kenneth Rexroth, Ginsberg, Warren Tallman, Lucia Berlin, and others. Repeatedly, she speaks to the generosity and graciousness of Kyger, whose invitation to Hawkins to read with her at Intersections on July 29, 1971, in San Francisco, provided for Hawkins's debut, assisting her to "come out of the closet," as she characterized publicly becoming a writer.

Hawkins's personal website, www.bobbielouisehawkins.com, contains extensive bibliographic information, reproductions of some of her drawings and paintings, a detailed list of her public readings and performances, audio recordings, and home movies. The last were filmed by Hawkins from 1962-1965 and then assembled as a continuous film by PennSound.

Hawkins was the recipient of a National Endowment for the Arts fellowship in 1979 and a Briarcombe Foundation residency in 1983. In the later part of her career, she performed with folk and jazz singers Terry Garthwaite of the band Joy of Cooking and Rosalie Sorrels.

Hawkins had four children: Kirsten Ann Hoeck and Leslie Karen Hoeck (now deceased), and Sarah Hall Creeley and Katherine White Creeley.

We conducted the interviews on July 5, 2001, and June 24, 2002; our questions and comments have been removed, and Hawkins's remarks have been lightly edited at the sentence level for readability. The 2002 interview contained many retellings of the events described in the 2001 interview, so materials from the two sessions have been consolidated to produce a single coherent narrative. Although like home movies themselves, especially from the mid-twentieth century, the interview moves with jumps and starts, tight close-ups and blurry panoramas, backs of heads obscuring one's view, unidentified characters hurrying away from the camera. It is for this reason that we've titled the interview "Home Movies by Bobbie Louise Hawkins" alluding to Hawkins's intimate, amateur films of the artists and others who comprised the

Courtesy of Naropa University Archive, n.d., photographer unknown.

mid-twentieth-century American poetry scenes that constituted her life. Hawkins's energy and story-telling acumen create the verisimilitude of the rolling movie camera recording her life's unfoldings, and we are indeed grateful to have experienced these literary "home movies."

The Early Years

"Bobbie has her own language; it's west Texas/California hipster—circuitous sentences and winding ideas, use of particular words, and cadence [....] you can hear it in her prose."
—Elsa Dorfman (*Elsa's Housebook: A Woman's Photojournal*, 4th edition n.p., 2017)

Writers and painters will often say that they knew at the age of eight or ten that they were that thing, but I didn't know what I was going to do. It was clear, though, that I was not in sync with Texas fundamentalist baptistry. My first intellectual argument was with my Uncle Maren when I insisted that men and women had the same number of ribs.

My relatives simply gave up on me. They loved me, but they registered that there was something patently wrong with me, although I think that when I was briefly preaching, when I was 12, it was because I couldn't see another place to go. Hellfire and damnation. I was strong on hellfire and damnation. A very easy topic, as topics go.

So I'd gone through the first and second grade the first year in school, and the third and fourth, the second year. Then I was in the fifth grade, and we moved to New Mexico, which probably had a much stricter set of [academic] standards than I was accustomed to. That was also the year my father left. Everything went weird. And I passed conditionally.

I also developed something like a heart murmur, and I started going to a Catholic school that gave you points if you went to mass. So I always went to mass because I was really strong on points. But I loved it. A Mexican Catholic church is nothing like a Baptist church. I think it's the shape of the cross, and there's something about the air. To go in there and just sit with the candles going and all this gold. So it was clear that unless somebody put an ad in the paper saying, "Do you want to travel?" I was not going to go anywhere.

I graduated from high school when I was 15. By that time, I was doing a lot of reading. As soon as I was told how to read, I could do it. And my mother read masses of gothic horror, astounding stories, amazing stories. I was reading Olaf Stapledon's *Odd John* [1935; *Odd John: A Story Between Jest and Earnest*; Stapledon, 1886–1950.], a classic of science fiction writing. It was the first time I came across a utopian theory and superior persons finding themselves able to communicate across territories; they all had different capacities. I read that, and I felt absolutely kindred to it. I also read all the Oz books [Notably *The Wonderful Wizard of Oz* (1900) considered America's first true fairy tale, by L. Frank Baum, 1856–1919] and all of Richard Halliburton [American travel/adventure writer, 1900 – presumed dead after

1939]. I discovered him by myself just by scanning libraries. He told a simple form of history intended pretty much for bright adolescents. It gave me an alternate world. There are many different reasons why persons become writers, but one of those is definitely people who are desperate have to save their own lives and have to do it forthrightly and have no equipment, no input, where they are. They find books. And then there is the implication of rooms with people in them talking like this, which was a salvation. By reading, I was convinced that there was a place in the world for me to be if I could figure out how to get there. But that feels rather like Yeats, who at one point said, "I have met women who wanted nothing better than to be married to a poem." I mean that I wanted nothing better than to live in a book!

So then I knew I was going to be an artist. It was just a question of what kind.

Now I had a large vocabulary as a reader, but I was extraordinarily shy, so I didn't have a developed diction. What I did when I was 15, I stopped [at an art center in Albuquerque where] this man was proposing a repertory company of actors for radio soap opera. He would train these people, and everyone would be paid union minimum, which in Albuquerque was a phenomenal salary. So I auditioned and was accepted as the youngest member of this company. This was exactly the place for me to stop being shy with my voice and to get rid of my Texas accent. That's an interesting business about people who are moving up the social scale: the question of who chooses to lose their accent, to shift their accent. I made that choice, whether it demonstrated a lack of character or not. In this projection, which I had, there was to be this woman walking forth in the world, sophisticated and worldly, and able to be there, and she did not have a Texas accent! I couldn't imagine anyone being erudite in Texas.

Then I lucked out in high school my senior year, and I had a teacher who thought I was talented. Now I took two art classes that senior year with this guy, and in one of them I was acting as his assistant with younger students and in one of them I was simply working on drawing and painting. And another girl and I were his star pupils, so he would take us up to wherever shows were happening in Albuquerque, like at the Johnson Gallery or the university, and we would meet professors who were teaching painting and calling themselves artists. We felt very honored. Plus I instantly adored all that manipulation of color and all that. In fact, I'd made a pact with myself at the age of 16, which was that at the age of 30, if I were not actively living the life of a real painter, I would kill myself. Your classic 16-year-old contract.

But before I got out of high school, I was very confused, and whether I had an intelligence or not hardly entered into anything. So, for instance, I started skipping classes. French class and English class. The only classes I was consistently showing up for were the art classes. Now at one point I realized that I was about to not graduate, so I went to an advisor and told him I'd been skipping classes. I felt that I needed someone to intercede, to intervene, to be the adult telling them that they should let me back in. So, he did that, and he started giving me IQ tests, and he was the first person who ever told me that I was distinctly intelligent. It was extraordinary just

BOBBIE LOUISE HAWKINS   Johnson and Grace

Photograph by Elsa Dorfman.

to hear that whatever my confusions were there was some baseline there. What then happened, which was a serious piece of luck—there was this awful English teacher who was going to flunk me, and my adviser explained to her at length that it was very important that I get this degree. I graduated from high school with a D- in English!

[Later], at one point, Michael McClure who taught at California College of Arts and Crafts [now California College of Arts] in Oakland went on sabbatical, and I took his job while he was gone, and at one point with all these painting students, I'm giving them reading assignments and discussing stuff. It's clear the very next time they come in that almost no one has done anything. And I say, "Okay, what's up?" and one of the students says, "You should be aware of the amount of dyslexia." I thought, "How interesting." And that would have been the same thing as my incapacities and confusions around arriving at a public language. An unusable language would obviously make me move straight over to painting. Also painting is so emotional. It's instantaneous emotion, and it lets you milk that and get the good of it, and it doesn't require words.

So, I decided that I'd go to university. I was 18 when I started. I took those entering tests, and my English score was so high that I was let off Freshman English entirely. But in my ongoing incapacity to behave socially—artists who can leave their hometown and go to New York! Or to a city!—I had absolutely no comprehension of how I might do that. It was completely out of the way; I just had none of the skills. I was living with my mother and stepfather, who were both very distressed because

I wasn't doing something straightforward like getting a job in a department store while I waited to marry someone. I tried to leave home briefly but it didn't work. I just didn't understand money at all; my assumption had been that [while at university] I would get a job and pay back the loan company and accrue the money toward the second half of the tuition. But I didn't do that.

Marriage, Travel, and Writing

So six weeks after I've started [at the university], this Dane [Olaf Hoeck] arrives [where I was working]. He was an architect in charge of an English firm's West African office in Lagos [Nigeria]. He pokes his head in and asks where the office is, and I tell him, and he goes to the office and comes back and says they've all gone to lunch and would I like to have lunch. So fortunately, I wanted to go to lunch, so I said, "Yeah." So we went to lunch and then he asked me out that evening. And then he asked me out the next day for lunch and proposed to me. I said, "But I'm not in love with you." And he said, "That's okay. That can come later. You have to get out of Albuquerque, New Mexico." And I kept saying no. I met him in early December 1949. So it was two nights before he was due to leave, and I found myself thinking if I don't do this, I don't know how to get out of here. But here was this person offering to do it for me. Like that line of Charles Olson's: "My life has given me its orders."

Olaf and I left Albuquerque in December '49 to arrive in Denmark. From there, we went to England thinking we were going to Africa, but he'd over-stayed his leave, so we were in England for a year. During that time I went to the Slade, it's part of University College London. I met Lucian Freud [British painter, 1922-2011]. I was the only student he spoke to. He didn't speak. At one point, going through the halls, he said, "Should we have coffee?" and I said, "Yes," and he walks on by, and the student I'm walking with said, "He talks to you!" and I said, "Yeah," and she said, "But he doesn't talk to anyone." I said, "What does he do?" and she said, "He stands behind people and emanates." And I thought, "What a ploy!"

But he and I would go to this Turkish coffee place, and he took me to the Leicester Gallery to a showing of Sickert [Walter Richard Sickert, British painter, 1860-1942] paintings that Sickert hadn't allowed to be sold during his lifetime. That was the only time I heard of Sickert, until years later, like 1959, going to the Bay Area and staying with Robert Duncan and Jess [Collins, artist and Duncan's lifelong partner], and I wasn't there more than three minutes when I flashed, "These are people who will know who Sickert was." They instantly filled me in on the whole story, like he did work for the *Yellow Book*; he was this or that kind of painter. Jess disappeared and came back with books in which there are paintings by Sickert.[1]

So then Olaf got with the Colonial Development Corporation, and we went to [Belize] and were there for two and half years. I'd gotten pregnant in London and arrived in Belize two weeks before my daughter was born. I think that was my major college because I met extraordinary, internationally travelled women. I learned to play canasta and bridge and tennis, and as soon as I got there, Olaf bought a sailing boat, a little 18-foot Seagull. So, we were racing once a month. I was in a book! I was in a book! But then it wasn't so specific that I was a character. It was simply that I was there. I was seeing things that were interesting. And people were saying things that were interesting. That was the difference. Suddenly I was in an educated British community [where it] is taken for granted that you say that thing you mean to say in exactly the words that work for it. Whereas in an American community, a young woman who is using precise language that lets the things get absolutely said is instantly suspect.

That sort of thing pretty much fed into *The Sanguine Breast of Margaret*.

[That book] is autobiographical in the sense that I know what happened. It isn't autobiographical in the sense that I cannot remember who I was. The minute I'm beyond any experience, I'm the person that I am now. So anything like that is an invention, and the closest one can get to its being, however much it's autobiographical, you are *fictively* inventing yourself. You're the person who is invisible. You get to see everybody else, and you're always back of the lens; you don't see you in context. When I think back, writing *The Sanguine Breast of Margaret*, that book began in 1969 and wasn't finished until 1983 because it was my first novel, and that was the thing I wrote secretly; I wrote a 100-page initial draft, which obviously no longer exists. Then it went through 17 drafts. In each draft as I would approach it, I would remember the persons who had been writing earlier drafts. I had to in some way regain that person within the context, and I simply couldn't. So I decided I was going to a hypnotist with a list of questions and a tape recorder. She would be talking to the person who was there then! And the tape recorder would register the answers, and they would feed into the book, so that things could be made clear. I wanted it to be real. In every single draft I wrote, every next draft, I became a little more apparent. Finally, it became my book and not the book of those men who were the strongest characters.

After Belize, we moved to Japan. And what he [Olaf] was doing was building fast, low-cost housing in South Korea for all those people who were living in cardboard boxes and down the hills.

In Tokyo, the community I had there let me down because it was mostly embassies, and Olaf at that point was with the United Nations, so it was those persons who if they had any skill at all, it was developing a vocabulary that let you say nothing. Diplomatic. I also had my second daughter in Japan.

I was writing at that time, though. We were skiing—he was skiing and I was making herring bone marks up the small hills— and there was an editor there from the *Stars and Stripes*, also a man named John [Jack] Sack [1930-2000], who incidentally was one of the people at the '68 Democratic Convention; *Esquire Magazine* sent a curious group of writers to that '68 convention. They sent Genet, and Jack Sack, and Ginsberg. Anyway Jack Sack was there, and I came to know this editor, in Tokyo, and I remember at one point I had a short story I'd written, and he'd asked me for it. And I gave it to him for the *Stars and Stripes*.

Then the marriage ended. I quit painting when the relationship with Olaf ended in Japan, and I came back to the states. Olaf was on a diplomatic visa and was completely aggravated that I'd gone, [so he] sent me no money. I [ended up] living in my mother's garage and paying her a hundred a month. My kids were in nursery school, not Salvation Army, but like that.

A part of what I thought I might do is sing in a night club, so I called the musician's union for a piano player and got Race Newton [American jazz musician and second husband of poet Lucia Berlin] who was meanwhile explaining to me that I did not want to sing in *any* nightclub in Albuquerque because they were all mafia. [Race] had these friends Buddy Berlin [American jazz musician and third husband of Lucia Berlin]. And Buddy and Race had been Creeley's two closest friends at Harvard. When Creeley's first marriage ended, when his romance with Martha Rexroth ended, and his teaching at Black Mountain ended, he came to New Mexico.

For me, it was purely and simply a matter of how do you live. I came from a working class family, so there wasn't some notion that there would be money hanging there in the bank. Except when I got with Olaf, of course. In [Belize], I had a cook, a maid, a laundress, and a nursemaid. In Japan, I had a cook and a housemaid. When I got back to Albuquerque, I had a garage and a job that paid me too little money, and it all pretty much felt the same—like getting on with stuff.

Creeley and Avant-garde Poets

The minute I sighted Bob, I just adored him. It was that classic whatever it was. It was late '56. We got together in late '56. Well, actually, maybe January '57. And then stayed together for 18 years. We were both just entirely too volatile. That relationship had massive collisions and all directions going in it.

But he and Max Finstein came by, and Bob asked if I had a place where he could sleep. Now he had an apartment of his own that was this gray adobe apartment in the back of an old adobe house. But, he asked me, and I said, "Absolutely," so he came and slept on this mattress on the floor in the living room. And then it was just that funny classic thing of he said there [would be] two nights before we could touch each other.

We moved from that house later to an old farmhouse, which was a great place to live—out in Alameda, New Mexico. Now at that moment in time, we had four kids. Because with Creeley I had two more kids. So we had four kids who were living in a four-room adobe house, but we had running water and a bathroom.

Now Bob was not famous. I mean, he was teaching Latin at a boys' school. But he wasn't famous publicly. He was famous among the people—[William Carlos]

BOBBIE LOUISE HAWKINS   Johnson and Grace

Williams, [Ezra] Pound, and [Charles] Olson, and [Robert] Duncan—all those persons. They knew each other, and they worked with each other.

I really resist the assumption that the women who were there and attended to the men were doing their own writing and were necessarily writers. I found that a nurturing environment. All those people were talking about writing, all these books were constantly coming to the house; every little magazine that got published, copies came to the house. I was absolutely learning a history of American writing as it existed at that time. We think that's important for students; it was certainly important for me. I just learned it from this other side! Well, the actual side, the people, not second-hand.

So shortly after Bob and I got together, Charles Olson had just put that time in San Francisco briefly, and he and [his wife] Betty were on their way back across country. He stopped and stayed with us for a while. When Sarah [Hall Creeley] was three months old, maybe a little older, [we] went to the Bay area, in late '57, and I met Ginsberg and Jimmy Broughton, Peter Orlovsky, Michael McClure, and John Wieners. At that moment in time, John was an absolute angel. Angelic personality. Just phenomenal—and that's when I met Joanne [Kyger]. I was meeting the people who would figure strongly in my life thereafter. That has to be counted as nurturing. They were or were not interested in whether I was or was not a writer; that meant nothing. I think my prejudice apropos this business of women wanting to be given the same scale as the men they're with, they still have to do the work.

Bobbie Louise Hawkins and Anne Waldman, July 7, 1990 (courtesy of the Allen Ginsberg Estate, photographer unknown).

Joanne was claimed as a protégé by both Jack Spicer and Robert Duncan. She was so impressive, and she was so good-looking. She was then a buyer for one of those downtown San Francisco stores...and you'd see her...the short hair cut...I remember her wearing a chiffon scarf with a little metal rose. She was just wonderful. And very funny. They called her Miss Kids. Joanne, like a twenties flapper, would get that kind of walk, and come in, like, "Oh, kids!" It was so funny. She was so funny; she was great. She continues to be one of the truly graceful people. I've had dinner at her house when she was, as they say, "on her uppers." I've seen her be really poor. And I've seen her have enough. I've never really seen her be rich, but when she has money, she's the same, just the same, just as gracious. I went to dinner at her house once and we ate beans and homemade bread and a salad and a bottle of wine—and it felt like a feast! It was just fantastic. She's one of the world's wonderful women.

I always did admire Diane di Prima [as well] because she grew up in millions of people. She grew up in a city locale [New York City]. She never, ever formed solitary habits. She lived her life in the middle of people. At one point, I remember when she and Alan [Marlowe] were at the Hotel Albert, and people would arrive and simply want to be adjacent to them. She would find out what their skills were, and if their skills fed to the Poets Press, or if they fed to one of her [other] enterprises, she'd have a room for them. At one point, she had one whole floor of the Albert, minus the ballroom, and then this guy arrived who knows how to run a printing press and she had the printing press, but doesn't have anybody who knew how to use it. So, she gets a room for this guy, and he's the printing press guy, and then she rents the ballroom. So they're doing printing in there, plus it's where they're stacking all the boxes of books, plus they're having readings. I mean, her resourcefulness. I met her when LeRoi Jones was LeRoi Jones [before changing his name to Imamu Amiri Baraka in 1965]. And we immediately hit it off. The funny thing is at one point she said to me, "I certainly never thought of you as being 'with' Bob." She's a good friend.

[But] it has always been my experience that the men I was with gave me the community I then was in. I learned a lot by being with the poets. I feel like I should write "A White Woman Among the Poets." But it was true that the poetry community was a community. If Bob had been a prose writer, I would never have met a community of writers. So that suddenly the fact that Bob was a poet among poets gave me friends and a community that was incredibly supportive.

I never had friends. Well, I mean, I have the friends who were at my twenty-first birthday party in [Belize]. Those friends managed to stay. [But] beyond that, all my friends are the ones I met with Creeley, and then of course there was that classic thing of the minute the relationship between Creeley and I ended, I lost fifty percent of the people who were my friends while I was with Creeley, but then there were the people who were my friends when I was with Creeley and were my friends later, like Joanne, like Joe Brainard, and Anne Waldman.

In fact, Bob and I were supposed to go to Naropa together one summer. [But] we took a year's trial separation, which is a euphemism that allows you to get out

BOBBIE LOUISE HAWKINS   Johnson and Grace

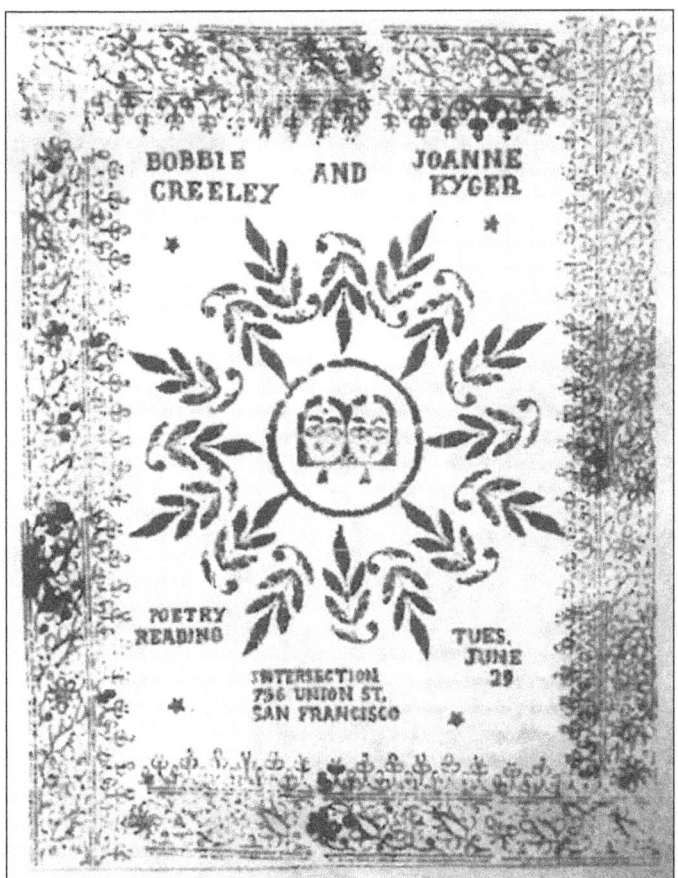

Flier for a reading at Intersection for the Arts in San Francisco on June 29, 1971 (courtesy of Elsa Dorfman, published in Elsa's Housebook: A Woman's Photojournal, *4th ed., Boston, MA: David R. Godine, 2017, n.p.).*

of there. The telephone rang, and it was Anne, and she said, "I understand that you and Bob have split," and I said, "Yeah," and she said, "Does that mean you're not coming to Naropa this summer?" I said, "I can't afford to come to Naropa for a hundred dollars, plus pay my ticket," and she said, "Oh, we'll give you a ticket and you can do an evening reading and we'll pay you." I got on the flier. I'll always owe Anne Waldman for that, in exactly the same way that when I did come out of the closet [about writing], sitting down on the beach at Bolinas with Joanne, and Joanne said, "I'm going to be reading at Intersection next month and I'm supposed to read with someone. Would you like to read with me?" My immediate response was, "You know, Bob hasn't given a reading in the Bay area in some time. I'd know he'd love to do it." She said, "I'm not asking you about Bob. I'm asking you about you. Would you like to read with me at Intersection next month?" This was probably '71. It was just when I was publishing these little books of poetry. So, I gave this reading with Joanne. My first reading, my first public reading was with Joanne at Intersection. My friends knew I was writing, but suddenly to be there, in the world as a writer, so you see there was in a sense a woman's support group.

The Vancouver Poetry Festival, 1963

Vancouver Poetry Festival, July 1963. Left to right top rows: Jerry Heiserman, Dan McCloud, Allen Ginsberg, Bobbie Louise Hawkins Creeley, Warren Tallman, Robert Creeley above Charles Olson; seated left Thomas Jackrell, Philip Whalen and Don Allen (courtesy of the Allen Ginsberg Estate, photograph by Allen Ginsberg).

Warren Tallman [American professor of poetry], who was wonderful, did this absolutely stunningly smart thing and decided they wanted to have a summer event. [Warren] wrote to Creeley, Olson, and Ginsberg to ask them if they would be free for three weeks and got affirmative answers. He then wanted to bring additional writers each week, so he asked Robert Duncan if he would be free the first week. Robert says yes. And Margaret Avison [Canadian writer] and Denise Levertov! At this point,

Warren Tallman says, "I've been in touch with a few people. We could get so-and-so, so-and-so, and so-and-so," and he told them the entire schedule.

There were 200 students. And he set up the format: it was to be Monday, Wednesday, and Friday. So there were these breaks in between, which was great, and he set it up so that way with three weeks, the students were divided into thirds and each one would spend a week with Creeley, a week with Olson, a week with Allen. And mornings the writers would be down front discussing their writing.

I've got this on videotape. I've got some great home movies, but first I'm going to make a documentary of them.[2]

So that was a great event. And there were nice things, like Ellen Tallman. She [was] one of the world's wonderful people (and incidentally went to school with Robert Duncan and Martha Rexroth and Don Allen). She had a particular knowledge of secondary drugs that deal with your body in different ways. So suddenly, here's Duncan, Creeley, Olson, Allen, and we're all crammed into the kitchen at the Tallman's. The talk is going all night, and then they're supposed to teach the next morning. There was a point when Ellen arrived in the kitchen at midnight, and she would go once around the room, saying, "And this one is for you...." She would go right around the room giving everyone a pill! When you took that pill, you had *exactly* 15 minutes to lie flat on your back where you were meant to sleep. It was great!

Berkeley Poetry Conference, 1965

Of course, Dick [Roshi] Baker [American soto Zen master] then chose to do it down in Berkeley. It was *very* expensive, and it didn't allow any space for the poetry student population in Berkeley who couldn't afford to hear this stuff. So—it was summer, the windows were open and the students started climbing in and sitting on the window ledges listening. Now there was a point when Olson, Creeley, and Ed Dorn said, "Okay, in through the window. Grab a[n empty] seat." [So one morning], here's Dick Baker looking incredibly authoritarian, his suit and his crewcut and statistics, and he launches on, "Of course, it's perfectly alright for you to have anyone sit in your classes that you know. However, your salaries are being paid by the persons who are paying for this event. If there are going to be people sitting in that room who don't pay it's only appropriate that those persons who are paying be given their money back. And if they're given their money back, that means we will not have the money to pay you for doing this." And Bob says, "Keep the goddamn money!" And Baker says, "Oh, well, you know, I have an appointment," and off he goes. They all had contracts, and he backed down. And those persons continued to be let in through the window to fill unoccupied seats.

[At that event] I remember Lenore [Kandel] and Joanne read together. Lenore, who was then the belly dancer for the Arab Club and the Israeli Club, was reading *The Love Book* [1966], which was an *incredible* breakthrough, as opposed to all of these so-called sexual, erotic writings by women where the primary thing being said was, "I'm really good in bed. Look at me. I'm talking about sex! Doesn't that make me interesting." Lenore Kandel's talking about fucking. And she was dressed in very ultra-high heels; fishnet black stockings; a mini skirt *that just* managed to make it below the crotch, very tight; a very broad patent leather belt, absolutely tight so the waist was minute. A tight sweater, so the breasts were seriously present. And her hair was a kind of pompadour and down. She's reading these poems and the whole audience went "God!" And then there's the intermission. And people were sort of leaving. I remember as I was leaving there was this man coming down the aisle like a Baptist confessional en route, and with his hand out, and as he goes past he says, "I *have* to touch that *woman*." She was a fantastic hit!

And then after the break, it was Joanne's time to read and Joanne read from *Tapestry and the Web* [1965]. That was after she and Gary had broken up. So, the very next night, I went out to dinner with Bob and Don Allen and Gary. We're sitting there and I say to them, "That was the first time I've heard Joanne read. She is *fantastic*." And both these men look at Gary! It's for Gary to say. Gary then says, "Yes, I worked with Joanne on it." I instantly just cut out. It was like, "Okay, I know this story. To hell with this one!" And I thought, "How ungenerous." These were men who would be pleased for their [male] friends; as their friends achieved different things in poetry, they would celebrate with them. Suddenly, it was as if anything that Joanne was, she was made by Gary. In fact, not even Jack Spicer and Robert Duncan claimed that! They never claimed that she was a poet because of them.

I mean, the one big drag with Allen was that as soon as he'd screwed some young man he'd instantly think it conferred genius on him. Boring young men got their lives destroyed by thinking they were geniuses because they'd fucked Allen Ginsberg. Spicer was the same way. That he would cultivate them, help them to write poetry. Maybe they were important. Most likely they were not. Even now, we don't know. I read their names, I reference their work but....Now Joanne is far more visible than some of the young men that Spicer cultivated with an intensity.

[Now] Lewis [Welch]. He's a classic instance of a man who did not get respected and got lost and killed himself. He was always so aggravated by the fact that Gary Snyder and Philip Whalen were being given all that attention, and he was saying, "Don't they realize there were *three* of us, there were *three* of us?" There was Gary who was making the biggest flash. And then there was Phil who was making this flash that was not as large as Gary's, but he had the scholarship and stuff. And Lew just was sort of in the backwash. Don Allen published [Welch's] *Ring of Bone* [1979], but [it] could have been published two years earlier.

BOBBIE LOUISE HAWKINS   Johnson and Grace

Early '70s

When we got to Bolinas, there was suddenly a writing community. And a writing community isn't all that interested in doing maintenance on the great men. It's much more interested in everybody having some kind of equal billing. And as soon as I was there I came out of the closet [about writing]. You get seriously warped when you stay in the closet as an artist. You think of yourself grandiosely in order to take up the slack. But it's unfair to feel superior to somebody else's event when you're secret, when you're holding it all back. I made that move, and it was healthy. And Joanna McClure said to me, "When you started doing that it gave me the courage to do it."

But in [1973, '74] I was writing secretly. I wrote a whole novel secretly when Bob and I were living in Eden, New York. It was pretty straightforward. I mean his take was, "I cannot live in a house with a woman who writes," was one thing. And

Joanne Kyger, Allen Ginsberg, Bobbie Louise Hawkins, Peter Orlovsky, Michael McClure, and Diane Wakoski at the Bisbee Poetry Festival in Arizona, August 1980 (courtesy of the Allen Ginsberg Collection, Stanford University, photographer unknown).

"everybody's wife wants to be a writer. If you had been going to be a writer you would have been one by now." It's like, well that's the advantage of being a writer, you get the serious whammies, like each thing straight from the throat. So we were just fighting about it.

What I would do is, twice a week Bob would go into Buffalo. I would wait half an hour, which meant he had gone beyond the point of no return. And then I would go to the typewriter, which had originally been my typewriter but became his typewriter as soon as we married. It was one of those beautiful little Olympias—those first Olympias in those lovely greens and browns; this was one of the brown ones. And I paid it out $5 a month, and instantly turned it over to Bob as soon as we got together. It felt normal to do that. Well, he would, on top of it, have stacked these things. So I would take these things and put them here in exact order, then I would take the typewriter to the dining room, then I would go into a closet and take this cardboard box out. So then I would have two and a half hours. Because he would be doing a class, he would be doing office hours, and he would be driving home for an hour. And then, half an hour before he was due back, I would take the typewriter, put it exactly where it was, put these piles back on it exactly. Now that included, and this sure feels to me like a feminist principle, that I was not to blame for this. That this was my decision, and the thing I was really acknowledging was that I didn't write well. I didn't have the energy to fight and to learn how to write. So the shot was I was going to not have the fights. And whenever he would go away to do readings and stuff, I would have more time and I'd work on it. And I finished a first draft of a hundred pages. It was unhealthy and made me schizophrenic.

It's the space. It's having the space. He thinks if I write I'll be referring to him and causing him to have to pay attention to it. So I thought if I can write the thing and it's there and it's clear that it took nothing from him, then it will be all right. But it wasn't. It really wasn't.

[But I kept writing] because I was getting good at it. And because I'm a talker. Writing is a great thing for talkers. It's how you get to keep talking when nobody's there. Plus I really believed it was gonna be a book. Now that book went through 17 drafts over a long period of time. Because each time I'd come back, a year would have gone by or something, I'd get a certain amount of it done and then time would go by. Meanwhile I was doing a lot of painting. I didn't have and I still don't have habits which cause me to think of an ideal, rather than what it is I can do. And the painting was public and open. I'd finish something and I'd pin it on the wall and it'd be sort of there. It didn't interfere with the house in the same way [that the writing did].

Meanwhile the guy—[this may have been John Martin of Black Sparrow Press]—who was one of the earliest editors for fiction in New York—at one point when he was staying with us for awhile, and I was telling him stories about my Texas relative, he said, "If you write those down, I'll publish them." So I wrote them down, but it was sort of like it might be all right because it was sort of like memoirs and not writing. And he published a few of them.

But he said, "I can't publish you because no one knows Bobbie Louise Hawkins. But what I can do is help you maintain your anonymity." Now this was before Creeley knew I was writing. "I can send poems from here [NYC] saying there is a woman here who I have met and this is her name and I can send your poems out to people." And he did. Meanwhile, I had a secret letterbox at Hamburg, New York, that I would do correspondence with John Martin.

I get really dragged by some guy who has achieved something, which one saw over and over and over again, young writers who'd be coming to see Creeley. They'd have their girlfriend with them and their girlfriend would be speaking in terms of needing to discover herself, and I would think, "Oh shit." When you have a person who's gone through the history Creeley has gone through and, in fact, because I took it personally and I had this idea that I was the only woman in the world who should be with him. I thought I was going to be there forever. That only lasted until it got bad. He began drinking a lot more and more and more. He stopped talking in a way that was interesting to me. It was just clear that there was a major vanishing return here, and at that point I started explaining that I wanted out. I just wanted out. I would give a perfectly good case, and then he would look at me and he would say, "Are you going to leave me?" And I would say, "No." We did five years of that. Your classic five years.

One of the things I'd really registered was that classic twist that I see with my students. You start to write it down and you go stupid. The words start to torque on you. [One day] I was sitting next to this [guy from] Georgia. I immediately recognize this guy because he's like my relatives. And he says, "What does your husband do?" And I say, "He's a writer." And he does this classic "well, I've got some stories you can take back to him." So, I sneak a tape recorder in on him. I have a tape recorder in the pocket of a jacket. And I have a wire that goes down the arm, and every time he's ready to lay out a story, I fiddle with the jacket—flip the "on" switch. And he started telling me stories. And I claimed it for my own. I thought, "There's no way I'm giving these to Creeley. I'm keeping these." So as I was writing them out, what I really got on to was that Southern thing that I'm convinced is why there are so many Southern writers. Southerners are talkers. And I registered that I was a good talker and a bad writer. And if I could just talk onto paper I would jump miles of bad writing. It was a huge breakthrough. I didn't tape myself, but I ran a tape recorder on all my relatives. When I started transcribing their stories, everything was fantastically edited because they were not telling the stories for the first time. They were telling stories that got edited because you look in somebody's eyes and see their face going dead and you cut to the chase.

Trying to get *One Small Saga* written, I couldn't get straight on the form. I was trying to put it into paragraphs and chapters and it just doesn't happen, it just didn't work. Finally, I decided I was going to take everything here and I got involved with

Photograph by Elsa Dorfman.

the left-hand margin as thrust. So sometimes you'd have something like this and it just runs on until it stops. But I didn't want them to do it run-on. I wanted it to start at the left hand margin. When I was typing out the whole manuscript, I then went through the whole manuscript with a red ballpoint pen and I put a dot next to every sentence I absolutely wanted to start at the left-hand margin. It's like there's some kind of underlying theme that you're not gonna get; it's like you can feel it but you don't understand. That's the underlying formatting for that, that I went through. When I got it, it was such a breakthrough that I was convinced that I was going to do it forever. But I never did it again.

Moving On

Here's a very funny Creeley story. In the late 80's, Anne [Waldman] decided one summer to honor Creeley. Lucia Berlin [1936-2004] had come to read at the University of Colorado and was staying with me. This thing came up about Creeley coming, which was before he and I had made our peace. Lucia says, "What are you going to do? Leave town?" I said, "No, I'm going to have the party! Sure, I mean, think of it!"

I had known Lucia when she was married to Race Newton, and they were living not six miles away from [me and Creeley] in a two-room adobe house. Lucia was 21 or -2 with two small kids. She met Race when she was pregnant with her second baby, the one that her husband walked out on. It was the classic business of her husband explaining that a domestic life interfered with his art. So, she wakes up one morning, and he has gone around the house during the night taking the things that mattered to him, packing his suitcases, and he's gone to Italy. She was writing what became *Angels Laundromat: Short Stories* [1981] at the time. Phenomenal. [Later] she said to me, "When I was working on the *Laundromat*, I gave some of those to Bob. And at one point when I was at your house and Bob drove me back home, I really wanted him to say something about the Laundromat stories." So, she asks me, "Do you remember that cottonwood tree?" There was one of those classic New Mexico giant cottonwood trees outside this little place [Lucia and Race] lived in. And she says, "We stopped in the shade of that cottonwood tree, and I'm waiting for Bob to say something about the stories, and Bob says, 'Lucia, be like that tree for your man.'" And Lucia and I looked at each other and we...just...broke...up! I said, "Do you think he ever has any major neurosis about thinking of these two women, both of whom he would have absented from literature forever if he'd been given the chance?" Both of them independently went on, got on with it.

[But] in terms of living in an enriched environment, which is where I was living with Creeley, when it ended, the news of what was happening, what was going down and interesting, was not coming into the house, and, boy, I hit bottom. But I didn't hit bottom around the thing of "Oh, god, this relationship should not have ended." I

IN THE COLONY 86

dience of silent spectators, her eyes walling in all directions, she removed the obeah.

* * *

On the second-floor veranda of the house across the street the two Delara girls and their mother had begun their day of slow rocking in the shade. Each was equipped with a rocking chair, a fan, and a glass of iced fruit juice.

The hotel manager, who was prematurely hired by the CDC and now had at the least two years of time on his hands, with salary, had begun to court the elder of the Delara girls.

The two girls had been kept drastically intact their whole lives against just such a possibility.

The manager was given a plan of behavior that must be adhered to.
His conduct was one side of a transaction. The other side was this young woman's guaranteed condition. She was untouched. She had never even been to a dance. She had never walked on the street without the company of her mother or her father.

The suitor found himself dancing a very courtly dance indeed.
He had to make a daily call in the cool of the afternoon and sit on the veranda with his beloved and her sister and her mother.
When the father came onto the porch the suitor would rise, shake hands all around and leave.
Two times a week he was invited to stay to dinner.
He brought flowers daily and candy for the mother on the days he stayed to dinner.

Page from One Small Saga.

just hit bottom suddenly [because] everything went away. And at one point, it was just patently clear: I thought, "If I don't begin to live a more interesting life, I'm going to die."

And that's when I asked [musicians] Rosalie [Sorrels] and Terry [Garthwaite] if they would like to travel, [to] work in a cabaret format. I said I want to be *out* there. To my amazement, they both said they wanted to do it because, of course, both of them had had a dozen records out and were well known. I had in mind four women, and the other one was to be Diane di Prima; it was to be two women writers and two women singers. Diane was up for it, but she was so busy we could never get together just to work through a semi-evening.

When we started touring, we were getting each one our own venues. Rosalie had all the folk stuff down; Terry had down all this jazz circuit that she traveled. Then I would have different places like, for instance, the Joseph Papp Theater [in New York City]. Usually we were in music venues. We'd arrived [and be announced as] Terry Garthwaite, Rosalie Sorrels, Bobbie Hawkins. Or at others, Rosalie Sorrels, Terry Garthwaite. So at some point, I go on stage, look at everybody and say, "I'm the third one!" The room would break up! Everybody knew those women, but who is *that*?

BOBBIE LOUISE HAWKINS

NEW One-Woman Show

LIFE AS WE KNOW IT

Joe's Pub
425 Lafayette St.
New York City

Monday, October 14, 2002

Performance will be at 9:30 pm

Tickets $10 at the door.

Information 212-539-8778

...sharp as splinters ...devastating and ironic ...
...beguiling, witty, and occasionally militant ...

Ms. Hawkins has written fifteen books and is noted for "a poignant thread of cosmic humor" in her work onstage and on the page. Past performances at venues as diverse as the Greek Theater's BREAD AND ROSES in Berkeley, the Quiet Knight in Chicago, the Vancouver Folk Festival in Canada, The Great American Music Hall in San Francisco, One World Poetry Festival in Amsterdam, the Canterbury Festival in England, and in New York City at the Joseph Papp Theater, Bottom Line and Folk City were acclaimed by critics.

"Talent, integrity and humor, Bobbie Louise Hawkins is a poet and storyteller of the first order; each of her performances here (Live at the Great American Music Hall, Rounder Records) reveals a different aspect of her gift for poetic diction and her unerring ear."
ROLLING STONE

"Her prose is vivid, tinged with sarcasm and wisdom . . . A writer with a distinctive and memorable style."
BOSTON SOJOURNER

". . . a composite of experiences causing an introspective look into one's own existence . . . A standing ovation when the performance was concluded."
TOLEDO - THE COLLEGIAN

"Her ear is exact- the dialogue is sharp as splinters, as devastating and ironic as any dialogue set down by Raymond Carver or Ann Beattie."
TORONTO GLOBE & MAIL

"Hawkins punctuates her stories with laugh-provoking one-liners, but much of the humor comes from the faithful observation of character and the plausible rendering of circumstance."
THE SAN DIEGO UNION

"Hawkins is keenly aware of the complicated vastness of even just one little human universe. Her sentences do not meet that universe head on but at a 'slight angle'.

Hawkins' writing participates in a tradition of American Modernism in prose that sometimes achieves an almost hallucinatory precision. A thoughtful artist's eye informs the writing."
THE VAJRADHATU SUN

"She excels at the short take, the oblique view, and the sort of incident that allows the storyteller leeway to expand, change and alter the fundamental nugget of actuality.

Her curious, witty and occasionally militant slants make her writing unclassifiable but altogether beguiling."
L.A. TIMES BOOK REVIEW

"Hawkins moves with apparent ease from tale to tale, suffusing each with irony, anger or love as the occasion demands. Pieces of varying length are juxtaposed and, once fit together, the life of a woman emerges."
PUBLISHERS WEEKLY

"Hawkins, a splendidly handsome figure, is a poet and writer of poetic prose. In a voice as beautiful and sensitive as a grand opera diva or the grandest of jazz singers, she reads from her works.

She is a priceless artist who captures in every line a past that becomes a slice of American social history."
SAN FRANCISCO EXAMINER

"Miss Hawkins is a superb impressionist as well as a salty prose writer of American miniatures, artful distillations of our humor and humanity."
NEW YORK TIMES

Publicity flier for October 14, 2002, show at Joe's Pub.

BOBBIE LOUISE HAWKINS   Johnson and Grace

Notes

[1.] The *Yellow Book* was a leading journal of the British 1890s. The magazine contained a wide range of literary and artistic genres, poetry, short stories, essays, book illustrations, portraits, and reproductions of paintings. Sickert's painting "A Lady Reading" appeared in #1 of the quarterly.
[2.] This project never materialized. The home movies are availabe on Hawkins's website.

Selected Bibliography

Own Your Body, Sparrow 15. Black Sparrow Press, December 1973.
Back To Texas. Bear Hug Books, 1977.
Almost Everything. Coach House Press, 1982.
One Small Saga: A Novella. Coffee House Press, 1984.
My Own Alphabet: Stories, Essays and Memoirs. Coffee House Press, 1989.
The Sanguine Breast of Margaret. North and South, 1992.
Bitter Sweet. Back cover endorsement by Anselm Hollo. Bijou Books, June 1995.
Fragrant Spring. Back cover endorsement by Lucia Berlin. Bijou Books, June 1995.
Sensible Plainness. Back cover endorsement by Anne Waldman. Bijou Books, June 1995.

REVIEWS

The Cambridge Companion to the Beats
Edited by Steven Belletto
Cambridge University Press, 2017

The Cambridge Companion to the Beats is a comprehensive collection of academic essays that covers multiple aspects of the literature of the Beat generation. The 18 essays in this volume reach well beyond the traditional triumvirate of Burroughs, Ginsberg, and Kerouac to explore the impact of other writers and artists, including women such as Joyce Johnson, Diane di Prima, Lenore Kandel, and Joanne Kyger, who have been seen as increasingly significant as purveyors of the Beat *mythos*. The collection also includes writers of color, particularly African American writers Bob Kaufman, LeRoi Jones/Amira Baraka, and Ted Joans. The compiler, Stephen Belletto, is an associate professor of English at Lafayette College, the author of *No Accident: Chance and Design in Cold-War American Narratives* (2012), co-editor of *American Literature and Culture in an Age of Cold War: A Critical Reassessment* (2012), and a former associate editor of *Contemporary Literature*.

The Companion starts with a comprehensive chronology of Beat publications from 1948 to 2016, listing primary texts as well as anthologies, journals, and criticism, and ends with an extensive bibliography of further reading. The chronology consists of publications by and about the Beats, including collections of Beat writing and also contemporary critical overviews of the Beats. The "Further Reading" list follows a standard approach, listing academic studies of the Beats alphabetically by author and providing publication information. The 18 chapters discuss the concept of the Beats, the relation of the Beats to later countercultural movements, Beat aesthetics, Beat literary history, three central Beat authors (Ginsberg, Kerouac, and Burroughs), the role of memoir in Beat writing (focusing on Joyce Johnson's *Minor Characters*, as well as works by other female writers), and issues of gender, sexuality, transnationalism, and race as they pertain to Beat culture. Final chapters explore Beat relations to Buddhism and Christianity as well as the impact of jazz on Beat aesthetics, and Beat intersections with visual culture, primarily cinema.

Belletto introduces the volume by noting the development of Beat scholarship and by working to expand the definition of Beat—or, alternatively, by asking whether "Beat" can be defined at all. Central to this discussion is a sense of "Beat" as a term that alludes to a secretive counterculture that, in fact, defines itself through this binary of inclusion/exclusion. Surveying 60 years of commentary on what constitutes "Beat," Belletto isolates such comments as "the Beats are at bottom about 'protest'—against what, exactly remains vague" (Belletto 11, citing Seymour Krim's 1960 anthology *The Beats*) and "The reaction of [Beat] writers has been against academism and formality, stiff prosody, controlled ambiguities, precise cultural references, lyrical suppression, and censored emotions" (Gene Baro, qtd. in Belletto 11). These observations lead one to see the Beats as leaning toward spirituality (though not necessarily formal religion) and political concerns that sometimes lead to activism. Thus Belletto mentions A. Robert Lee's stressing of "the relationship in the Beat phenomenon between art and politics, the power of the word and the power of the deed" (14). This spiritual/political tendency spills over into the international or transnational Beat scene through works of writers such as Andrei Voznesensky of Russia, Kazuko Shiraishi of Japan, and Simon Vinkenoog from the Netherlands, and other writers (Belletto 17).

Belletto's collection provides more than straight-forward homage to the Beats, even though the core Beats still retain in many ways the status generated by their elevation from 1950s pariahs to countercultural icons. Particularly critical are chapters by Ronna C. Johnson, "The Beats and Gender"; by Polina Mackey, "The Beats and Sexuality"; and by Todd F. Tietchen, "Ethnographies and Networks: On Beat Transnationalism." In her chapter on the Beats and gender, Johnson criticizes the "Beat binary" encoded in a "masculine Romantic protest against restraint" that categorizes gender as "a bivalent system, a dimorphic construction of complementary but opposing female and male positions" (163). Johnson locates an original "dogmatic universalized masculinity" in the works of Ginsberg and Kerouac, a nascent backlash of "white femininity" expressed in the 1960s by female Beats such as Sheri Martinelli, Brenda Frazer/Bonnie Bremser, and Lenore Kandel, and a movement to see their response "misogynistically eradicated" in works such as Burroughs's *The Wild Boys* (163-164). Johnson highlights this frontal attack on gender equality by incorporating Kate Millet's assertion that "'misogynist literature' [read Burroughs] is 'frankly propagandistic' in its aim to keep 'both sexual factions' separate and unequal" (175). The counter-position to this assault appears in Bonnie Bremser's "*cri de guerre,* 'I embrace my prostitution'" (175).

In "The Beats and Sexuality," Polina Mackay argues that for the Beats, "sexual preferences do not point to...ethical choice," but are "fluid" and "tied always to political or social commentary" (180). Often (though not always; cf. Burroughs, again) these relations link sexuality and spirituality. Mackay argues that female Beats especially find "sexuality and its potential for breaking the rule of gender conformity...[to be] a significant trope" (186). Tietchen's chapter, "Ethnographies and Networks: On Beat Transnationalism," describes much of the Beat international experience or "Beat ethnography" (209) as "imperial adventuring" (212). Such "imperial adventuring" is evident in Burroughs's "fascination with sexual slavery and...persistent fantasies of kidnapping an indigenous boy," as well as in "the promise of exotic drugs in more licentious environments" that motivated both Burroughs and Kerouac (214). Tietchen uses the term "slumming" to describe much of the Beat interaction with the Third World and the fellaheen (215), and even calls Kerouac a "*flâneur,* a footloose observer seeking out bliss in this or that contact zone" (218). In contrast to these tendencies, Tietchen points to Ted Joans and the surrealist aspect of the Beats that links this movement to anticolonialism and *Négritude*. Still, he concludes that "[t]he range of issues and perspectives comprising Beat literature remains a sobering reminder that transgressive art and literature can often be as socially regressive as it can be socially progressive" (222).

In aesthetic terms, some critics see the Beats as exemplars of impulses of their time that connect them to a larger sphere of an ongoing revolution in letters, art, and society. Thus the Beat œuvre continues the original impulses of Dadaism and Surrealism (see Nancy M. Grace's "The Beats and Literary History: Myths and Realities," especially pages 71-73), with surrealism described as internationalist, mainly through its impact on *Négritude*. Grace notes Ted Joans's work here, as she does Kerouac's explorations of spontaneous prose (73), while Joans himself asserted that the "Beat Generation owes practically everything to surrealism" (qtd. in Tietchen 220). Grace links the Beats to the Modernists, debunking the fallacious assumption that the Beats were anti-intellectual (68-74). The Modernism link is central to her discussion of Ginsberg's indebtedness to William Carlos Williams. Indeed, in his chapter, "Allen Ginsberg and Beat Poetry," Erik Mortenson goes so far as to say that "Howl" "owes its existence to Williams's mentorship" (79), in that it fuses Williams's "short, imagistic line" with a Whitmanesque structuring of the poetic line (80). Grace also notes Kerouac's "admiration for Joyce" and points out that Kerouac filters "Joycean interior monologue and wordplay through the conversational style of Neal Cassady's epistolary voice" (70). At a level more contemporary to the Beat experience, Michael Hrebeniak in "Jazz and the Beat Generation" presents an impressive discussion of the intersections of jazz, particularly bebop, and Beat literature, particularly with regard to Kerouac, whose phrasing Hrebeniak argues often mirrors the riff and return of the bebop artist constantly improvising over a melodic base. Throw in the abstract expressionism of Jackson Pollock and others and we see an emerging aesthetic of unconstrained immediate expression as revealed in Kerouac's "spontaneous prose." This is discussed in Regina Weinreich's "Locating a Beat Aesthetic" and is also brought up in relation to surrealist psychic automatism by Grace (73), and in Ginsberg's dictum, "First thought, best thought" (qtd. in Hrebeniak 251).

Somewhat left out of this approach is perspective on Burroughs, whose experiments with cut-ups and fold-ins seem in some ways to set him apart from the other Beats. Oliver Harris writes in "William S. Burroughs: Beating Postmodernism" that "Burroughs seems to exist in parallel universes as a Beat [and] as a postmodernist" (127), and claims that when Burroughs began his experiments with these methods in Paris, he was effectively "splitting himself off from his Beat associations. Corso, Ginsberg, and Kerouac were all mystified and appalled by his new methods" (133). Thus, Harris claims, "Beat Studies no longer needs Burroughs to firm up its legitimacy, [while] Burroughs' reputation is such that his scholars can now ignore a field of dubious relevance" (127). Burroughs's distinctiveness seems especially noticeable in Weinreich's chapter on Beat aesthetics, in which Kerouac and Ginsberg's focus on spontaneity and "sketching" get full treatment, while Burroughs seems underserved.

Kurt Hemmer makes up for the lack in "Jack Kerouac and the Beat Novel," in which he supplies an illustrative comparison of extended "prose" passages from

Kerouac, Ginsberg, and Burroughs (116-17). The passage from Burroughs pre-dates his cut-up period but helps the reader hear the rhythmic unities that in the 1950s bound these authors' works—the breathlessness of the short image, the spontaneity and speed of the *now* as each author relays it. Hemmer further underscores this unity by appending a passage from John Clellon Holmes's *The Horn*, where the sense of immediacy, or much of it, is missing (117). More to the point of Burroughs's aesthetic adherence to Beat principles are David Sterritt's comments in "The Beats and Visual Culture." As Sterritt puts it, "[t]he cut-up's great advantage, [Burroughs] asserted, is the room it allows for *spontaneity* and *happenstance*; the best writing 'seems to be done almost by accident,' and here was an invaluable tool for writers who previously 'had no way to produce the accident of spontaneity'" (267; my emphasis). Reading Sterritt's argument, one might argue that the cut-up is a way of eliding suspect personality infected by the word virus, which sabotages spontaneity via preprogrammed words, potentially rephrasing Ginsberg's "first thought, best thought" as "first thought, programmed thought." Still, Burroughs's experiments link him to postmodernism in ways that may explain why some authors describe him as increasingly separated from the Beats.

According to Brenda Knight in "Memory Babes: Joyce Johnson and Beat Memoir," interest in the Beats revived in the 1980s with the publication of Johnson's *Minor Characters* (1983), a "narrative of the Beat Generation with the stories of the women who were there" (137). The corrective presence of the female Beats has "challenged the conventional notion that the 'Beat boys' were the main attraction" (137-138). Johnson and other women of the period such as Elizabeth Von Vogt, Carolyn Cassady, Joan Haverty Kerouac, Edie Kerouac-Parker, Joan Vollmer Adams, Hettie Jones, and Brenda Frazer/Bonnie Bremser have written about their experiences with the Beats, demonstrating, as Anne Waldman has noted, that memoir is "the strongest literary genre by the women of the so-called Beat generation" (qtd. in Knight 144). The memoirs and (in Diane di Prima's case, "meta-memoirs") written by the Beat women as well as by Herbert Huncke, Harold Norse, and Neal Cassady give evidence to Knight's assertion that Beat writing "ripp[ed] twentieth-century American literature out of the safe zone and away from academic formalism" (148). Knight quotes David Barnett as saying, "[a]lthough some critics assert that the male Beat writers repudiated the memoir as a lesser literature, even Kerouac, nicknamed 'Memory Babe' for his feats of recall, intended all his works as a *"roman fleuve,* a memoir cycle woven into the mythic, wondrous tapestry of his life" (Knight 149). Given that Kerouac's main works are *romans à clef,* their connection to memoir and the overall confessional focus of Beat writing suggests an underlying urge toward embracing of this once-minimalized genre. Writes Knight, "[i]t is hard to know whether [reviewer] Gilbert Millstein would have announced a nonfiction version of *On the Road* as the epochal book that sparked a new generation....It is fitting and fateful that Kerouac's partner at the time [of *On the Road*'s publication], Joyce

Glassman (later Johnson), would elevate the memoir to a higher form and bring forth a chorus of voices previously unheard, the women of the Beat Generation" (149).

Central to this casting of women as purveyors of the Beat ethos, and most recognized as equivalent in stature to the male Beats, is Diane di Prima. In "Beatniks, Hippies, Yippies, Feminists, and the Ongoing American Counterculture," Jonah Raskin asserts that di Prima "played a leading role in the political and spiritual rebellion of her contemporaries...pointing out that women usually did the cooking, shopping, cleaning, and more" (41). Raskin, who wishes to confront "the challenges that have faced historians and biographers...of the Beat Generations" (36), stresses the permutations that keep defining, refining, and transforming the countercultural impulse that was launched by the Beats. Di Prima's 1969 publication *Memoirs of a Beatnik,* Raskin claims, "signaled yet another tipping point in the Beat narrative" with its "feminist parody of male pornography" (42). Even though Raskin claims that "the initial Beat bubble burst" as early as 1951 (37), when Burroughs fled Mexico after killing his wife, the Beat impulse continued into the 1960s and beyond; Raskin cites Ginsberg as a major influence on Bob Dylan (39) and points to the presence of Ginsberg, Burroughs, and Gary Snyder at events such as the 1967 San Francisco Be-In and Gathering of the Tribes (Ginsberg and Snyder), the 1968 Democratic National Convention protests (Ginsberg and Burroughs), and the 1969 Chicago Eight conspiracy trials. Hilary Holladay, in her chapter on "Beat Writers and Criticism," goes so far as to say that "the feminist, gay, and lesbian poets of the 1970s and 1980s are...part of the continuum in which the Beats have a significant place" (151).

Beat artists' travel to India, Cuba, South America, the Mahgreb, and Europe profoundly affected the works of many of these writers, and in some cases (as in that of LeRoi Jones, aka Amira Baraka) had an impact on them in ways that led them away from their affiliation with the Beats. After visiting post-revolutionary Cuba, Jones distanced himself from the Beats and became a leading figure in the Black Arts movement, espousing Black Nationalism (A. Robert Lee, "The Beats and Race" 201). For Lee, Jones's *Preface to a Twenty Volume Suicide Note* already points toward this departure, suggesting that "'Beat'...is sedimented in whiteness" (200). Snyder, on the other hand, disappeared for years in a Japanese monastery to study Zen. John Whalen-Bridge, in his chapter "Buddhism and the Beats," suggests that the Beat immersion in Buddhist beliefs and practices is part of a long, ongoing introduction of Buddhism into American culture, starting in the early- to mid-nineteenth century. Much of this spiritual introduction consisted of trendy popularization that tends to obscure the serious nature of the enterprise. Whalen-Bridge points to the "camp aesthetic" that underlies much of the Beat attempt to transmit Buddhist beliefs. Camp is defined as "a sympathetic form of parody" reflecting Susan Sontag's description of comedic camp as "an experience of underinvolvement, of detachment" (qtd in Whalen-Bridge 232). Thus much of the working of Buddhism into Beat literature—Whalen-Bridge cites, in particular, Ginsberg's "Wichita Vortex Sutra" and Snyder's "Smokey the

Bear Sutra"—involves an underplaying or semi-satiric commingling of enlightenment with entertainment, as in Snyder's playful but austere assertion that "Smokey the Bear will illuminate those who would help him; but for those who would hinder or slander him, HE WILL PUT THEM OUT" (qtd. in Whalen-Bridge 234).

Though Snyder, like Jones, distanced himself from the Beats, albeit for different reasons, the inclusion of his work seems inevitable given his association with Beat writers after the 6 Gallery reading, described by William Lawlor in his chapter, "Were Jack Kerouac, Allen Ginsberg, and William S. Burroughs a Generation?" (30-31), and his portrayal as Japhy Ryder in *The Dharma Bums*. Still, Snyder's distancing and move into environmental activism may explain why several important studies of his work are not mentioned in the text or in the anthology's bibliography. One might easily consider *Gary Snyder's Vision* by Charles Molesworth and various books by Patrick D. Murphy important enough for inclusion. Also prominent in their absence are Snyder's important essay collections, particularly *The Practice of the Wild* (1990), *A Place in Space* (1995), and *Back on the Fire* (2007). These texts may have seemed to Belletto too removed from the Beat emphasis to merit inclusion.

Kirby Olson's chapter, "Beat as Beatific: Gregory Corso's Christian Poetics," addresses the important though sometimes overlooked impact of Christianity on the Beats: "Although the Beats tend to be associated in popular imagination with Eastern religions such as Buddhism, forms of Christianity also played a prominent role" (242). Olson points out Kerouac's linking of *beat* to *beatific*: "in a state of beatitude, like St. Francis, trying to love all life, trying to be utterly sincere with everyone, practicing endurance, kindness, cultivating joy of heart" (qtd. in Olson 242). Other prominent Christian Beats that Olson mentions are Philip Lamantia, who "wrote on Catholic themes throughout his lifetime" (242), William Everson, who spent 18 years as the Dominican friar Brother Antoninus, and Mary Norbert Körte, a "Beat-associated poet" (242) and a nun for 16 years before leaving her order to engage in political activism. Olson argues that "Corso's work points a way out of identity politics and toward reclaiming a basic patriotic belief in God and the United States…he opens the way toward revalorizing the American Christian tradition" (248).

Given the religious emphases in these later chapters, readers might understandably wish for an exploration of the impact of Judaism and Jewish thought on Beat culture. Ginsberg's "Kaddish" and the long standing (though non-Beat) trope of Zen Judaism might pave the way here, as could Kenneth Rexroth's explorations of the Hassidism of Martin Buber, with its emphasis on the distinction between "I/Thou" and "I/It" relations, the development of the prophetic voice in Beat writing and its relationship to the Old Testament, and the rebellions of Joyce Johnson and Hettie Jones against their strict Jewish upbringings. Other important Beat writers whose work might show the impact of Judaism include ruth weiss (whose family fled the Holocaust) and Elise Cowen.

So what is Beat? We can end this review by returning to its beginning, or at least the work of its compiler, Steven Belletto. In his chapter, "Five Ways of Being Beat, Circa 1958-1959," Belletto focuses on two works by Tuli Kupferberg that "explicitly theorize the meaning of Beat" (93). Kupferberg starts this way:

THE SUBJECTS OF BEAT poetry:
1) sex
2) narcotics & alcohol
3) jazz
4) insanity
5) the Negro[.] (qtd. in Belletto 93)

Later claiming that "[t]he Beats link themselves & are linked to the new rising energies of Africa & Asia, to the primitive current life-loving peoples of Mexico & the Caribbean" (qtd. in Belletto 94), Kupferberg—and Belletto—make clear the allegiance of the Beat to something beyond mainstream culture, bringing us back to the trope of inclusion/exclusion that Belletto describes in his introduction to this comprehensive volume. Belletto later looks to di Prima to find a part of this ethos determined by "the bohemian ideal of 'cool'" which (at least for Beat women) "is as normative as the square injunction to monogamy" (104), and which for women, according to Ronna C. Johnson, made them "de facto collaborators with their own oppression, because the essence of cool is the appearance of passivity, indifference, and lack of emotion" (qtd. in Belletto 104). Despite this tendency in the Beat world toward an apolitical coolness—an attitude that for many would be exploded by the chaos of the 1960s—the Beats, in their turning away from mainstream America and their frantic dashes around the continent and then the globe, "were invested in criticizing the 'social lie,' whether with respect to the mandates of bohemian versus mainstream culture or in connection to questions of racial or gender norms" (Belletto 108). Thus we come full circle, having submerged ourselves in the wealth of perspectives presented in this comprehensive volume.

—Allan Johnston, Columbia College–Chicago and DePaul University

Hip Sublime: Beat Writers and the Classical Tradition
Edited by Sheila Murnaghan and Ralph M. Rosen
The Ohio State University Press, 2018

The Beat Generation, once referred to in the popular press as wild-eyed seekers, bongo beaters, and eschewers of all things establishment, was in fact a differentiated group. The full range of Beat writers comprised different races, genders, sexual orientations, and vastly varied artistic styles, yet they generally shared one thing. Whether formally educated or self-taught, they read widely. In many cases, this led to contact with the literature of the classical world and allowed for its influence on some Beat writers. Edited by Sheila Murnaghan and Ralph Rosen, both professors of Greek at the University of Pennsylvania, the literary critical academic essays in *Hip Sublime: Beat Writers and the Classical Tradition* explore this influence, bringing together for the first time both classicists and Beat Generation scholars in a cross-disciplinary effort. Some writers who are generally considered outside of the Beat literary movement (but are shown to have shared the ethos and sensibility and in some cases the milieu of Beat writers) are included here; in general, the essays collected in this volume demonstrate how the classical world affected the art of Beat and Beat-affiliated writers.

Though *Hip Sublime* includes chapters on Robert Creeley, Ed Sanders, Robert Duncan, Kenneth Rexroth, and Charles Olson, this review focuses on a representative group of core Beat writers to demonstrate *Hip Sublime*'s ambitious thesis. In part, the book's effort to show that the classical world was a touchstone and inspiration for the mid-twentieth-century avant-garde in American letters reveals a paradox at the heart of Beat generation art. In the 1950s, the Beat writers' concern for an American civilization that was becoming increasingly culturally shallow and politically controlled by Cold War fear spurred their antipathy to the status quo while frequent news reports of atomic bomb threats created an atmosphere of existential uncertainty that resulted in their inclination to fall back on personal experience and the present moment. However, as Stephen Dickey, Sheila Murnaghan, and Ralph M. Rosen point out in their introduction, the Beats were inspired "across a long Western and increasingly Eastern tradition" underscoring the truth that "they were often reaching for exactly the kind of stability and continuity that they thought they were casting off" (1). From this perspective, the Beats are not necessarily rebels against tradition but seekers after an earlier tradition grounded in sincerity and stability.

As some of these writers sought innovative literary inspiration, they were brought back to the classical literature that comprised parts of their formal and informal educations. The paradox of throwing away tradition while embracing its foundational bits is brought out in clear relief in the essays on Gregory Corso, Phillip Whalen, Diane di Prima, and Charles Bukowski, which I discuss below. Corso, a visionary and highly original poet, found direct inspiration from classical writers and cultural forms. Whalen, the noted "Beat Buddhist," found fruitful syncretism in a poetics of East and West. Di Prima's pan-cultural and highly imaginative and individualistic art also included classical influences. Bukowski, noted chronicler of society's down-and-outers, was inspired by the neoteric (an appreciation of the everyday and nontraditional subject matter) Roman poetry of Catullus (c.84-c.54 BCE). The discussion on Bukowski is also fruitful as it complicates the definition of "Beat" literature and demonstrates how a more elastic understanding of this group can be fruitful for literary studies.

But what did Beat artists discover in the world of traditional and culturally hegemonic Greco-Roman letters? Given such an eclectic group of writers, results varied. The collection's title suggests part of the answer. For some of these writers, the classic tradition proved to be both hip but also transcendent. In the classical world, the Beats discovered a pure and refreshing wellspring to nourish western art, which contrasted sharply with a post-WWII America of consumerism and commercialized art.

Gregory Corso, the self-taught prison inmate who impressed poets from Randall Jarrell to Allen Ginsberg with his poetic voice and imagery and what Ginsberg perceived as his spiritual gifts, was the Beat poet most clearly inspired by classical themes. Corso was abandoned as a child and later incarcerated for three years at Clinton State Prison in Dannemora, New York, before his release at age 20, when Bunny Lang sent him to the Poets Theater in Cambridge as a guest of her friends at Harvard College, where he decamped to the Widener Library and read the classics. These episodes provided him with important connections to ancient western sources of knowledge. In *Hip Sublime*'s opening chapter, "Beats Visiting Hell: *Katabasis* in Beat Literature," Stephen Dickey explains that Corso had embarked on a mythic journey of *katabasis*, a term Dickey defines as "coming down":

> the term can mean any descent—as an army to the sea, or a wind down a mountain—though more specifically it is used of a journey to the land of the dead as iterated through ancient epic—*Gilgamesh, The Odyssey, The Aeneid*—then Christianized in literary treatments of the Harrowing of Hell and, in its most sustained elaboration, Dante's *Inferno*. (16)

The Beat underworld included life on the road, the harrowing experiences of men such as Corso and Neal Cassady, substance use and abuse, and identification with the "other" America of the marginal and dispossessed. Like Homer's hero Odysseus, many Beat poets were there to witness their own journeys and to tell the tale of it in poetry and prose.

Beat movement writers' affinity for Greek and Roman literature takes some unexpected turns. Among the group's most ardent Buddhists, Phillip Whalen was also influenced by Greco-Roman letters as demonstrated in critic Jane Falk's chapter, "Phillip Whalen and the Classics: A Walking Grove of Trees." The grove of trees in the title symbolizes Whalen himself as a one-man academy, as well as "the olive grove owned by Academus, reputed to be the site of Plato's Academy" (212). Having assumed the role of the academy in his own person, Whalen saw his poetry as didactic and also as bringing about a synthesis between East and West, the occidental cultural and religious traditions and the Zen Buddhism to which he devoted his life. Like Gary Snyder and Ginsberg, Whalen appreciated the works of Ezra Pound, a poet steeped in the classical tradition. Whalen refers most explicitly to classical literature in his poem "The Slop Barrel: Slices of the Paideuma for All Sentient Beings" (1956). Pound derives his neologism Paideuma from the Greek *paideia,* meaning the rearing and education of an ideal member of the polis. Pound explained Paideuma as the complex of ideas from a given time. Whalen shows his syncretic project in this poem, which looks to a new poetic vocabulary that, according to Falk, "juxtaposes several layers of language: American speech and slang ('Native Speech,' as he titles several 1963 poems); Western (often classical); and Eastern (often Buddhist) terms and concepts" (216).

From the responsible and serene Whalen, the collection moves to the inveterate drunkard and chronicler of the grotesque, Charles Bukowski. In her chapter, "Radical Brothers in Arms: Gaius and Hank at the Racetrack," Marguerite Johnson, who teaches ancient history and classical languages at the University of Newcastle in Australia, shows Bukowski to be a fellow traveler of Catullus, a poet of the late republican period of Rome. Catullus recounted his personal life and experiences in poetry, disregarding the historical themes often associated with classical verse. Bukowski read Catullus in translation and referred to him on several occasions in his poems in what Johnson calls a "dialogue." Johnson counts three approaches Bukowski takes in respect to Catullus: direct address, direct reference, and imitation. Johnson points out the ways that "Bukowski establishes and reaffirms a bond between himself and Catullus, albeit grudgingly at times. He casts Catullus as his own Furius or Aurelius; his *contubernalis,* the object of ridicule and attack but also affection and admiration, depending on context and state of mind" (98). A connection between Catullus and Bukowski across space and time is charming and at once humorous and sincere, as the curmudgeonly Bukowski discovers a kindred soul in a tunic.

Johnson assures the reader that Bukowski was, in fact, a Beat generation figure, despite Bukowski's assertion that "art dies in crowds" and his general antipathy towards the movement expressed in correspondence. But she has enough evidence to make the case that Bukowski is close to the Beat movement and its exemplars. She points out that City Lights published Bukowski, and *Outsider* magazine published him with Lawrence Ferlinghetti, Ginsberg, and Burroughs. More importantly, however, Bukowski had a Beat sensibility in his poetics, which included "free verse" and an "anti authoritarian" stance. Johnson concludes that Bukowski was an "outsider beat" as well as a "beat materialist" like Neal Cassady, in the sense that he was beaten down by life and had to work to support his art. His was not the mystical vision of a wandering poet, but rather the embodiment of a guy who had to work at the post office. The grit of Bukowski's writing comes from its realism, its view from the street, at the bar, and among the working class milieu.

Bukowski expressed his admiration for the ancient poet:

> I like your way, Catullus, talking about the
> whore who claims you owe her money, or
> that guy who smiled too much—must have cleaned
> his teeth with piss, or how about the poets
> come with their blameless tame verse, or about
> how this guy married a slut. (101)

For Johnson, this poem, "what have I seen?," is evidence of Bukowski's familiarity with the Catullan oeuvre and his understanding of the neoteric style that Catullus represents. Catullus could also be downright lascivious, a trait that matched Bukowski's own inclinations. Johnson finds that "Bukowski, the beaten down Beat, is drawn to the low-life cast members of Catullus's poetic dramas, seeing in them, perhaps, the down-and-out men and women of Los Angeles who were neighbors, coworkers, gamblers, sex workers, and drunks" (102). Johnson's chapter convincingly builds connections between the ancient world and the modern mid-twentieth century avant-garde.

As it was for Whalen, syncretism was also at the heart of Diane di Prima's poetics. In their chapter, "Troubling Classical and Buddhist Traditions in Diane di Prima's 'Loba,'" literary critics Nancy M. Grace and Tony Trigilio locate a "confluence of revisionary spiritual poetics" that combines many traditions and mythological models inspired in part by Jungian psychology. *Loba* is an epic work in progress that has been published in two editions (1978 and 1998). It is a western epic, akin to Homer and the "tale of the tribe," as Pound called the classical epics. In this case, according to Grace and Trigilio, the tribes in question constitute the 1960s countercultures of "Beat/Digger/Hippie familia" (227). For di Prima, the one influenced "casts a selective light on the influencer" (227). As a poet, she appropriates the classical tradition, for her artistic goal, as explained by Grace and Trigilio, to explore a central question of the depth psychology of Carl Jung: "What myth are you living?" *Loba* comes from a "multivalent lineage" of diverse inspirations that di Prima reimagines and refashions, making them her own. Loba, the name for a goddess, is perceived by di Prima across cultures as "Native American (e.g., Loba, Canyon Lady, Spider-Woman), conventional Christian (e.g., Eve), Gnostic (e.g., Eve, Sophia), Buddhist (e.g., Tara, Prajna), Hindu (e.g., Kali), Middle Eastern (e.g., Ishtar), and Greco/Roman (e.g., Athena, Persephone, Calypso, Aphrodite)" (229). Grace and Trigilio see the epic, long-form poem as a version of "feminist revisionist mythmaking."

With *Loba*, di Prima morphs and recontextualizes her varied subjects and classical allusions, rendering them ahistorical and emancipatory. Her manipulated "classical narratives serve to restage female identity as subject rather than object through an emphasis on the female body thriving in its outsider relationship to masculinized religious cultures" (229). Grace and Trigilio show that di Prima's bravura artistic effort and creativity are at the heart of her use of classical texts for her twentieth-century western and American purposes.

One may wonder about *Hip Sublime*'s overall argument. Have the authors succumbed to cherry-picking Beat texts to bolster their own theories about the Beats and the classics? Fortunately, no. Understanding more clearly the multiplicity of classical influences on this diverse group will reward study of the Beat art movement. Also, these essays portray the writers discussed in this volume from fresh perspectives. Whalen, for example, a man associated with Beat Buddhism, is shown to be a writer strongly influenced by the Greco-Roman tradition; Bukowski, the poet of L.A.'s underrepresented lower classes, is seen as a fellow traveler of Catullus and an outlier Beat poet. Running through the text is the common thread of conflict between the poetic depictions of Beat life versus the conformity of post-WWII America. Here is perhaps the greatest lure of the classical world. Its expression of the heroic ideal stands in stark contrast to the mundane world of everday jobs and domesticity that the Beats either renounced or struggled to reconcile in their lives and work.

—Michael Amundsen, Arizona State University

The Spiritual Imagination of the Beats
David Stephen Calonne
Cambridge University Press, 2017

History has treated the Beats more kindly than seemed likely in the 1950s. What was once seen as a manifestation of juvenile delinquency, or as a form locked in the moment of McCarthyism and bop, has become institutionalised: many English literature programs now offer classes that focus on or that include Beat movement writers. David Stephen Calonne's *The Spiritual Imagination of the Beats* (2017) is representative of the current recognition of the erudition and sheer breadth of knowledge of its subjects. Like other recent studies, such as Nancy M. Grace and Jennie Skerl's *The Transnational Beat Generation* (2012), and Sheila Murnaghan and Ralph M. Rosen's *Hip Sublime* (2018), *The Spiritual Imagination of the Beats* recognizes that what is a quintessentially American movement, whose roots lay in Transcendentalism, Jack London, jazz, and movies, is both informed by global literature, religion, philosophy, and culture and has a legacy in many international as well as American art forms. Calonne's project is driven by a desire to identify the "intense and continual religious quest" pursued by the Beats in multifarious ways (vii): his concern is with how each of the writers he approaches constructed their own highly personal set of beliefs, which they deployed in their attempts to resist or transcend hegemonic American culture. Thus, for example, Gary Snyder "has explored both Native American and Buddhist spirituality," incorporating "these traditions within his own ecological poetics" (163). While such a starting point is hardly radical, Calonne's originality resides in his particular interest in the legacy of hidden religions and religious subcultures whose adherents were often persecuted by the dominant world religions such as Christianity, Islam, Judaism, and Buddhism.

Calonne draws on Lynn White's "The Historical Roots of Our Ecological Crisis" (1969) to support Snyder's contention that Christianity and the capitalist system it created is, at heart, a religion that is indifferent to nature and incompatible with the sort of environmentalism he saw in Native American mythic cycles and the iconography of, among others, Buddhism's Shingon school (164). The key with Snyder and the 10 other Beat or Beat-inflected writers Calonne examines is how each creates a "synthesis among a variety of spiritual traditions" without stooping to cultural appropriation (173), so that daily life becomes inseparable from spiritual growth. In Snyder's case, according to Calonne, this means that "one should commit oneself completely to each moment as it unfolds," giving it "our full attention and just do[ing] what is required of us, what is before our nose to do, without losing ourselves in thoughts of past or future: pursue right livelihood, do your duty, your *dharma*" (173). While Calonne does not fully develop the significance of this decision, it is a choice that places Snyder (and other Beat poets, such as di Prima) at the heart of a tradition of American non-conformism, from antinomianism through Transcendentalism to 1960s counterculture, that rejected hegemonic models of selfhood based upon consistency, acquisition, and adherence to the law.

Calonne applies this approach chapter-by-chapter to the following figures: Kenneth Rexroth and Robert Duncan; Diane di Prima; Bob Kaufman; Jack Kerouac; Allen Ginsberg; William S. Burroughs, Gregory Corso; Philip Lamantia; Philip Whalen; and, finally, Gary Snyder. Thus, his project plants its roots in the San Francisco Renaissance, although it acknowledges European influences in D. H. Lawrence (1885-1930), Antonin Artaud, and W. B. Yeats. From this initial premise, *The Spiritual Imagination of the Beats* is constructed around six interrelated themes, as follows:

> (1) the Beat discovery of the hidden religions and the way their friendships and discussions with one another evolved through agreement and controversy over spiritual questions; (2) the ways conventional faith—attending church, for example—was replaced by an emphasis on individual mystical experience unmediated by institutions; (3) the elements that constituted the Beats' individual orientations and the ways specific thematic concerns were continued from one author to another; (4) the phenomenology of visionary experiences through natural means as well as entheogens; (5) the critiques of right-wing evangelism such as Bob Kaufman's Dadaist satirical poems […]; (6) and finally, the ways Beats mobilized their spiritual ideas in the service of political and ecological goals. (12)

Calonne is, in many ways, well placed to undertake such a book: he holds a long-term academic and personal interest in William Saroyan (1908-1981), whose vernacular-infused, semi-autobiographical tales of American rootlessness position him as a proto-Beat, and he is the author of *Bebop Buddhist Ecstasy: Saroyan's Influence on Kerouac and the Beats* (2010). Calonne has also written biographies of qua-Beat writers Henry Miller and Charles Bukowski, as well as editing four volumes for City Lights of Bukowski's writings. His account of growing up with (and within) the California counterculture of the 1960s and 1970s and of his own history of reading both Beat and world literatures also places him as a figure with a foothold in the Beat universe. This location does, however, also hint at one of the limitations of *The Spiritual Imagination of the Beats*: the Beat canon that he constructs seems deeply conservative as well as under-researched, containing few, if any, innovations on the constitution of the movement.

While he suggests—erroneously—that di Prima has been "scandalously ignored" (14), and includes her in part for this reason, there is no sustained mention of any of the other female Beats whose work has been recognized in recent years by scholars such as Nancy M. Grace, Ronna C. Johnson, Amy Friedman, Kurt Hemmer, and Mary Paniccia Carden. Likewise, while the featured authors, unsurprisingly, represent a range of ethnic, religious, and sexual identities, the fascinating chapter on Bob Kaufman's mix of jazz with Buddhist and Dadaist sources is the only one to look at an African American writer. In the conclusion to the chapter on Ginsberg, Calonne notes that Ginsberg "would become a kind of active manager of the Beats, for he tirelessly helped in placing their manuscripts with publishers" (104), and it is this community of Ginsberg affiliates that serves, largely, to define *The Spiritual Imagination of the Beats*' canon of Beat literature. It is worth noting the gulf between this version of Beat and that found in *The Cambridge Companion to the Beats*, also published in 2017, edited by Steven Belleto. The latter is not only much more wide-ranging in its coverage of topics such as race, gender, sexuality, and popular culture, but also in its inclusion of major female writers such as Anne Waldman (1945-) and Joyce Johnson (1935-), the first who Calonne does not mention and the second who Calonne identifies only as Kerouac's sometime girlfriend (79).

Calonne is also, disappointingly, relatively uninterested in form. *The Spiritual Imagination of the Beats* focuses on Beat "themes" and "concerns" (14, 15), rather than on how the hidden religions shaped the formal aspects of the writers' work. While there are passages such as those on Saroyan's influence on Kerouac's style, and on "Ginsberg's yoking of the *mantra* to poetic performance in order to achieve specific political ends" (103), these are subsumed within a narrative that is more concerned with analysis based on comparative trivia: for example, the results of William S. Burroughs's derivation of insect imagery from Mayan mythology, which he fused with the knowledge he gained as a bug exterminator in Chicago, and how these contributed to his "desire to show us creatures who live under rocks, the forms of life people prefer to ignore and pretend do not exist" (112). For Burroughs, this is the world of addicts and homosexuals, those who have been rejected by wider society and have turned to, or created, an "underground" world with an at best tenuous connection to the "reality" inhabited by others (112).

Calonne's study refutes any suspicion held by lingering doubters that the Beats were uneducated philistines: what emerges, instead, is a community who—like their Transcendentalist precursors a century before—"were united in their disaffection for conventional belief systems, [yet] also had sharp disagreements" (15). That said, each of the writers discussed here shares a fascination with "*lore*—not *belief* or *faith*, but rather a treasure chest of cultural topoi with which to stock his [or her] imagination" (125), characteristics that Calonne attributes specifically to Gregory Corso and Robert Duncan. It seems impossible, at times, to prove that the Beat writers he studies had read the particular texts that are identified as precursors, influences, or guides: this is unsubstantiated overreach. More important, as Calonne concludes, is the fact that the Beats and the countercultures that followed "sought to resurrect a mode of being *before* modernity had closed the doors of perception and to re-find a lost unity of Self and Cosmos" in order to "arrive at the point where 'art' and 'religion' would no longer be categories separate from life, no longer 'subjects' to be studied at university but rather actually lived out in daily experience and tied to the goals of social and political revolution" (179). While this is a valid claim,

Colonne misses the historical and cultural contexts that the Beat writers emerged from and helped to create: such searches are apparent both in the mid-nineteenth century writings of Melville, Thoreau, and Whitman, and in the literary modernism of Cather, Hemingway, and Pound.

Writing this review on the day that the passing of Al Hinkle (1927-2018) was made public serves as a reminder that the heyday of the Beats was a long time ago. Hinkle was the last surviving figure to have been fictionalized as a major character (Ed Dunkel) in *On the Road*. It is now around half a century since Neal Cassady and Jack Kerouac died, and more than 20 years since the deaths of Ginsberg and Burroughs, and the political and spiritual messages delivered by the Beats seem more relevant than ever. Calonne concludes his book by reminding us that the Beats "sought to decondition themselves from superficial values of a society in which they felt radically homeless," a quest that, as he puts it, "seems as relevant as ever" (179-80).

—Chris Gair, University of Glasgow, Scotland

Works Cited

Belletto, Steven, editor. *The Cambridge Companion to the Beats*. Cambridge UP, 2017.

Calonne, David Stephen. *Bebop Buddhist Ecstasy: Saroyan's Influence on Kerouac and the Beats*. Sore Dove Press, 2010.

Grace, Nancy M. and Jennie Skerl, editors. *The Transnational Beat Generation*. Palgrave MacMillan, 2012.

Johnson, Ronna C. and Nancy M. Grace, editors. *Girls Who Wore Black: Women Writing the Beat Generation*. Rutgers UP, 2002.

Kerouac, Jack. *On the Road*. Viking, 1957.

Murnaghan, Sheila and Ralph M. Rosen, editors. *Hip Sublime: Beat Writers and the Classical Tradition*. The Ohio UP, 2018.

White, Lynn, Jr. "The Historical Roots of Our Ecological Crisis." *The Subversive Science: Essays Toward an Ecology of Man*, edited by Paul Shepard and Daniel McKinley, Houghton Mifflin, 1969.

REVIEWS   Field

The Routledge Handbook of International Beat Literature
Edited by A. Robert Lee
Routledge, 2018

In "Aftermath: the Philosophy of the Beat Generation," first published in 1958, Jack Kerouac explained how he and his fellow travellers were "prophesying a new style for American culture, a new style (we thought) free from European influences..." (48). During his life Kerouac maintained a deep reverence for American culture and love for his country—even as he became an international countercultural icon—while over the last 20 years or so the wider work of the Beat Generation has undergone a critical expansion. As A. Robert Lee argues in his Introduction to *The Routledge Handbook of International Beat Literature*, "Time has long installed 'The Beats' as a familiar, even fixed, pantheon" (1), and the work of the original triumvirate—Kerouac, Allen Ginsberg, and William Burroughs—has gained a kind of countercultural canonicity, aided by the contributions of other leading Beat players, among them Gregory Corso, Lawrence Ferlinghetti, Neal Cassady, and Gary Snyder. As Lee points out, however, in recent years the field of Beat Studies has widened the scope of critical inquiry beyond the usual suspects, as well as bringing the contributions of female, African American, and LGBTQ Beat poets and novelists to light. Contemporary scholarship has also explored the Beat Generation as a transnational phenomenon, examining the ways in which these writers played a central role in the global counterculture. "Beat, in other words," Lee reminds us, "has long moved on not only from the one pre-emptive canon but also from the one geocentric location" (15).

In works such as *Beat Generation Writers* (1996) and *Modern American Counter Writing: Beats, Outriders, Ethnics* (2010), Lee has led the critical charge in scholarship that seeks to enlarge the Beat canon and attendant criticism. In his work on the Beats, Lee has paid close attention to the input of African American writers, in particular Bob Kaufman and Amiri Barka, as well as to writers he calls "Beat Speaking Women": Diane di Prima, Joanne Kyger, and Anne Waldman. Lee has also explored the impact of the U.S. Beats across the globe in Russia, China, and Japan, his work foregrounding and complementing *The Transnational Beat Generation* (2012), edited by Nancy M. Grace and Jennie Skerl, a volume which opens out Kerouac's vision of the Beats to something far beyond a new American style.

As Lee makes clear in his Introduction, *The Routledge Handbook of International Beat Literature* does not attempt "to offer a reception study (Ginsberg as heard and read in the U.K., Europe, or Japan, Kerouac ancestry in France, or Burroughs amid drugs and the composition of *Naked Lunch* in the Maghreb, or the [Beats in Cuba])" (3). Rather, *The Routledge Handbook of International Beat Literature* focuses on writers from outside of the United States—including England, Scotland, Canada, Western and Northern Europe, the Mediterranean, Russia, Scandinavia, Finland, Greece, Turkey, the Maghreb, Japan, and China—whose work demonstrates a kinship or sympathy with the Beats. In this respect Lee's volume builds on "Global Circulation," the final section of Grace and Skerl's *The Transnational Beat Generation* which examines the influence of the Beats in the United Kingdom, Vienna, Prague, Greece, and Japan. That Lee was able to gather over 20 emerging and established scholars from over a dozen countries is testament to the growing international community of Beat scholars, underscored by the European Beat Studies Network, which formed in 2012.

The Routledge Handbook of International Beat Literature is an ambitious volume. The premise is straightforward—to map the sphere of influence that the Beat generation had on literatures across the globe—but in so doing, it raises a number of provocative questions. Was there, in fact, a coherent Beat message, sensibility, spirit, or style in the United States? And either way, which aspects of the Beats were used and adapted by writers across the globe? Or is it the case that the Beats' iconoclasm—their association with the counterculture and their disregard for social mores—inspired writers to challenge censorship and to innovate their respective national literatures? Is there a danger in eliding the counterculture with the Beat generation so that every underground movement is perceived as influenced by, or in some way connected to, the Beat Generation? Why were some cultures influenced more by Burroughs than Kerouac, and what does this tell us about respective cultural and political epochs? With respect to non-English-speaking countries, what role did—and does—translation play in the ways in which Beat writers have been received? And to what extent is the influence of Beat writers across the globe little more than a variant on the familiar story of U.S. cultural imperialism?

The most insightful chapters grapple with at least some of those questions. In "Beat Britain: Poetic Vision and Division in Albion's 'Underground,'" Luke Walker, writing from the U.K., charts the sometimes uneasy relationship between the Beat generation and their British counterparts, pointing out that "we need to be alert to the dynamics of American cultural dominance in the post-war years, and the ways in which this cultural presence operated on both mainstream and 'underground' British culture" (48). While some British writers, notably Michael Horovitz, welcomed the influence of Beat writers, Ginsberg was at times dismissive of his British counterparts, observing that "even the supposedly avant-garde poets...write, you know, in a very toned-down manner," elsewhere referring to their "dim diction" (47).

In "Étes-Vous Beat? Contemporary French Beat Writing," Peggy Pacini from Cergy-Pointoise, France, deftly outlines the history of French writing inspired by Beat writers, while raising "the genuine question as to whether there is such a thing as a French Beat generation or simply overlapping transatlantic activities and experimentations" (89). Tracing the significance of poets Jean-Jacques Lebel and Alain Jouffroy, Pacini questions whether "the residency of Ginsberg, Corso, and Burroughs in the Beat Hotel at 9 Rue Gît-Le-Coeur in the late 1950s might have given the promise of fostering more connections with a younger generation of French poets. In fact, it did not" (89). As Pacini observes, the late translations into French of major Beat works contributed to "the missed connections to the Beat Hotel period" (91).

Beat-influenced French writing, with a few exceptions, stemmed from the French émigré Claude Pélieu who moved to the United States in 1963 and the painter Brion Gysin, Burroughs's long-term collaborator.

One of the strengths of this collection is how the volume tracks the post-war literary history of countries in relation to the Beats but also the wider counterculture, from Alexander Trocchi's relationship with Scottish Beat-influenced literature to the Greek island of Hydra, a gathering point for writers such as Canadian Leonard Cohen and Australian journalist George Johnston, author of *My Brother Jack* (1964), a novel that probes social and cultural issues and is considered a classic of Australian literature. In "Children of Anarchy: Shoulder to Shoulder with the Italian Beats," Maria Anita Stefanelli from Universitá Tre Roma in Italy explores the convergence of various anarchist movements, the impact of American popular music, and the instrumental work of key individuals, among them Fernada Pivano and Gianni Milano. Jaap van der Bent, a pioneer of transnational Beat scholarship formerly from Radboud University Nijmegen in the Netherlands, traces the well-known figure of Simon Vinkenoog, one of the performers at the International Poetry Incarnation in London in 1965, as well as the Dutch poet Cornelis Bastiaan Vaandrager, whose work was influenced by Burroughs. In "German Beats: Friendship and Collaboration," Alexander Greiffenstern, who lives and writes in Germany, reminds us of the importance of Carl Weissner's translations of Beat writers and associated authors, among them Burroughs, Ginsberg, Bob Dylan, and Harold Norse, while chronicling a coterie of German writers influenced by Beat artists, including Udo Breger and Wolf Wondratschek. The volume includes fresh insights into the Beat influences on French-speaking Wallonia and Brussels, as well as Austria, but the collection also succeeds in shedding new critical light on countries not usually associated with Beat writers, among them Poland, Finland, and Russia. The final two sections include essays on Greece, Turkey, Morocco, Japan, and China.

In shifting the gaze of Beat Studies away from the United States, *The Routledge Handbook of International Beat Literature* demonstrates the ways in which the Beat generation was much more than a national phenomenon, illustrating the ways in which the work of Kerouac, Burroughs, Ginsberg, and other Beat writers intersected with, tapped into, and kick-started a global network of underground literature and art. The collection is not only an in-depth account of the Beats' transnational reach but also an invaluable account of postwar global counterculture. Many of the essays introduce intriguing countercultural figures who are not usually associated with the Beat pantheon. As Lee acknowledges in the introduction, the list of countries and cultures explored is not exhaustive, but by gathering together an impressive roster of international scholars, *The Routledge Handbook of International Beat Literature* opens up discussion of this field with verve.

—Douglas Field, University of Manchester, United Kingdom

Works Cited

Kerouac, Jack. "Aftermath: The Philosophy of the Beat Generation" (1958). *Good Blonde and Others*, edited by Donald Allen. City Lights Books, 1993.
Johnston, George. *My Brother Jack*. Collins, 1964.

Women Writers of the Beat Era: Autobiography and Intertextuality
Mary Paniccia Carden
University of Virginia Press, 2018

Mary Paniccia Carden's book represents a breakthrough of sorts in scholarship on Beat generation women because she frames her justification beyond simply bringing to light previously neglected women writers of the era. That undertaking of recovering women writers has been a worthy one (for example, see Johnson and Grace's *Girls Who Wore Black: Women Writing the Beat Generation* and *Breaking the Rule of Cool: Interviewing and Reading Women Beat Writers;* see also essays by Helen O'Neill, Jane Falk, and Amy Friedman as well as several anthologies) that has formed the foundation on which further work, such as this study, rests. The broader questions that *Women Writers of the Beat Era* engages are to be found in the book's subtitle, *Autobiography and Intertextuality*, and are taken on with a seriousness and complexity that go beyond the object of study to potentially provide paradigms for study of intertextuality and life-writing *tout court*. Although the ultimate meaning of "intertextuality" ends up relying on already-trodden ground in work on Beat-era women writers (that is, some of the "intertexts" referred to comprise extant scholarship or the contemporaneous clichés that most recent work on Beat women writers has been at pains to debunk), this book provides a significant contribution to literary scholarship as a study of a distinct group of women characterized by their countercultural community and historical postwar era.

In chapters on many of the major figures in the subfield of Beat women writers—Diane di Prima, Bonnie Bremser (Brenda Frazer), ruth weiss, Joanne Kyger, Joyce Johnson, and Hettie Jones—Mary Paniccia Carden examines how each writer, in one or more genres—poetry, fiction, correspondence, but above all, memoir—writes with, through, and against trite portrayals of Beat women, trite expectations of women during the early Cold War decades, and the impossibly contradictory expectations their Beat menfolk had of them. Carden demonstrates through these women's own writing, through her writing about their lives, and also through careful analysis of the ways their publishers marketed them then and now through book design and other paratextual materials, how they worked within considerable constraints both external and internal(ized) to become free and fully-actualized subjects of their own lives as much as was possible then, as much as is ever possible. Most were college-educated, upwardly mobile, with aspirations beyond the proverbial "MRS Degree," but also often yearning for fulfilling heteronormative relationships, though these relationships carried with them many remnants of patriarchal expectations, even if the trappings were superficially different. As Hettie Jones memorably and unapologetically asserted at NYU's "The Beat Generation: Legacy and Celebration" in 1994, "Yes, okay, so it was sexist, but anything was better than death in the suburbs!"

To unpack a bit the key terms of the subtitle: given the Beat penchant for emphasizing the extremes of life experience from ecstasy to utter abjection as legitimate and indeed preferred fodder for imaginative writing (and indeed almost de rigueur for achieving that gold standard, "authenticity"), compounded with relatively recent feminist scholarship that has emphasized "life writing" by women as a way of rectifying previously socially-imposed silences, autobiography should be a natural topic of investigation at the center of the intersection of Beat literary and feminist scholarship. However, the second matter of the subtitle's focus, "intertexuality," has a complex and rich relationship to autobiography that problematizes naïve notions of authenticity that imagine the latter as unmediated by previous textual endeavors. Lives are made intelligible by their interpellation into the already-extant world of texts available for narrative ordering of biopolitical phenomena experienced at the personal level, so any new expression of the "self" is always already a collage of what Carden calls "pre-texts." This is clearly an issue for women associated with the Beat generation, because a script has already been prepared for them, as Johnson and Grace have noted, as "girls who say nothing and wear black" (Kerouac, "Origins" 569), as amanuenses for their male counterparts, as semi-embodied beings who both facilitated (in "helping" roles) and obstructed (as gendered symbols, willy-nilly, of domesticated resignation to a conformist regime) these men's rise to literary fulfillment and fame. The "pre-texts" through which they are obliged to filter their experiences both do and don't "fit," as Carden demonstrates through careful readings of the life-writings, be they poetry, memoir, or fiction.

Extrapolating from conventional meanings of "intertextuality" into a multi-dimensional understanding of how life experience itself as well as its reproduction and representation in "life-writing" is constructed by pre-existing social conditions, this book re-imagines a dynamic intertextual practice and process: practice, because there is agency in these women who write; and process, insofar as the mutually generative and productive relationship between life and writing, between experience and representation thereof, takes on a life of its own, controllable by no one single force, be it historical, agential, or circumstantial. In the case of this volume, the stakes are a bit more circumscribed; by "intertextuality," the author here means not only that the writers grapple with social scripts that have been implicitly or explicitly written for these women, but also the ways in which they have been already depicted in or erased from the texts generated by and about their more famous male counterparts. Carden refers to these various pre-existing discourses (on young women in the 1950s, on the Beat generation, in previous relatively dismissive Beat scholarship and media coverage of the Beats) as "pre-texts."

There is an interesting issue with autobiography, however; minoritized people, including women, are presumed by a white mainstream to write *only* as witnesses or subjects. That is, all of their writing is assumed to be "life writing," as if they had no imaginations. Thus, the assumption by the press and public that the madwoman Lula in Amiri Baraka/LeRoi Jones's *Dutchman* was based on Hettie Jones implicitly diminished Baraka/Jones's capacity for both inventive mythmaking and broader social commentary (see Hettie Jones's 1990 memoir, *How I Became Hettie Jones*). It is a grave injustice to minoritized subjects' creative talents to assume their fictional art to be autobiographical. Beat writing actively valued and promoted life-writing and life-as-writing under the banner of "authenticity." Allen Ginsberg's brilliant interjection of the phrase "this actually happened" into one of the lines of "Howl" is both a strike in favor of this documentarian strain and a radical break with traditional notions of imaginative writing, i.e., "Don't break the fourth wall." There is a curious contradiction to be investigated here between the (mostly) white Beat writers' demand that "authenticity" line up with "autobiography" and the limiting of minoritized writers to writing *only* from life experience, a contradiction echoed in the author's claim, seemingly indebted to Susan Stanford Friedman's writing on autobiography (such as "Women's Autobiographical Selves" [1998]), that women are more often drawn toward life-writing because it allows them to shatter socially-constructed myths about the notion of "Woman." And this puts the (white) women writer subjects under investigation here in a curious position; the writing that is of most interest to Carden is their "life writing," that is, the writing from which we can gain the most insight about "what it was really like." Although I welcome further studies of their imaginative work that eschew entirely recourse to their status vis à vis their male associates (there is an increasing amount of work of this kind, cited by Carden, such as, for example, Linda Russo on Joanne Kyger), this volume, in its nuanced understanding of the vagaries of autobiographical genres and strategies, makes an important move toward complicating that genre.

One such instance of complication is the first substantive chapter, in which Carden compares Diane di Prima's two autobiographical works, *Memoirs of a Beatnik* (1969) and *Recollections of My Life as a Woman* (2001), published 32 years apart, to demonstrate the many factors and vectors that shape the presentation of a unified self implicitly promised by the genre. Although it is generally acknowledged that the first is a highly fictionalized bit of erotica solicited by Maurice Girodias for Olympia Press and written for money, Carden does not dismiss it so easily; she reads it with and against stereotypes of Beat women, not faulting it for its failings in terms of veracity but looking at how its construction of a female bohemian life compares with the later one to show how the two works, juxtaposed, perform multi-textured accounts of "truths." Carden places the chapter on ruth weiss in a context of "consociation," a term Carden gets from Anne Waldman's introduction to Brenda Knight's *Women of the Beat Generation* (1999, xi) and which suggests a shared but diffuse group affinity rather than a set of close acquaintances and colleagues. (Waldman cites Clifford Geertz's use of the term, who in turn got it from Alfred Schütz.) This chapter is a welcome addition to the growing secondary literature on weiss, whose life epitomizes a kind of life-as-art totality; her live "jazz performances" long pre-date the current spoken-word poetry development, and even seem to have evolved completely independent of the much-bruited 6 Gallery reading in which

Ginsberg would appear and, according to the Beat world legend, single-handedly initiate the extravagantly-rendered live poetry performance. The chapter on Brenda Frazer/Bonnie Bremser, one of the most haunting and compelling of all Beat writers, takes seriously the raw, ambivalent play of "selves" in the memoir *Troia* (1969), which documents the author's entry into the terrifying world of sex work to support her husband's writing and his addictions, leading them to give up their infant daughter for adoption. Frazer/Bremser's writing was undertaken, like her sex work, for her husband's benefit to entertain and titillate him while he was in prison. She remains for me one of the most important and enigmatic Beat writers.

Carden's attention to Joanne Kyger's 1960-1964 journals, published much later as *The Japan and India Journals, 1960-1964* in 1981 and then reprinted in 2000, reveals a now well-known abusive side of her then-husband Gary Snyder, as well as Kyger's acutely articulate and self-aware account of the crazy-making double demands of the mid-century, middle-class (white) American woman writer: that she be interesting, creatively motivated, and intelligent and also that she never, ever, for fear of fatal consequences, relinquish timely dishwashing in order to follow a creative urge. Kyger notes with knowing anger her erasure from accounts (by others and by her travel companions) of her Asian travels with Snyder, Ginsberg, and Orlovsky. Fortunately for us, she shed Snyder fairly early and blossomed as a writer in her own right. Joyce Johnson, whose memoir *Minor Characters* (1983) could be acknowledged as initiating interest in Beat women writers, plays with grace and humor the role of the good girl flirting ambivalently with her bohemian yearnings; unlike Elise Cowen (who does not come under close analysis here) and Bremser, Johnson pulls back well before approaching the brink of social death, perhaps precisely because of her acceptance of the contradictions about which she is so eloquent. Hettie Jones's two books *How I Became Hettie Jones* and *Drive* (1998), as the subjects of the final chapter, are analyzed via the concept of "contextuality," namely the variety of social and literary contexts in which Jones finds herself (in multiple meanings of that term). Experimenting with a variety of "alternative cultural positions" (a phrase that well-describes all of the women whose work is studied here), Jones exuberantly doubles down on her resilience across and through them all.

One element of the book worthy of further thought is that all of the women discussed (except Kyger, who died in 2017) are still living (as of this writing) and thus have had long lives in which to reflect (or not) on their role in what has turned out to be an important literary moment. Some, such as Joyce Johnson, have seen their independent literary and/or journalistic legacies eclipsed by their more recent roles as memoirists of the Beat era and, in Johnson's case, her relationship to Jack Kerouac, though that role has itself eventually led to a secondary interest in her other work. Others, such as Joanne Kyger, outlived others' fascination with their early years and have generated substantial oeuvres superseding their brief connection to a famous man. Still others, like Brenda Frazer, have moved deliberately into relative anonymity. ruth weiss could be said to have forged her literary career more independently of such associations, thus the linking of her name with the concept of "consociation." Di Prima and Jones, who have continued to write and thrive, are enjoying renewed attention; a comprehensive biography of di Prima is out now from Bloomsbury (*Diane di Prima: Visionary Poetics and the Hidden Religions* by David Stephen Calonne [2019]), and Jones has recently published her letters to and from Helene Dorn with Duke University Press (*Love, H: The Letters of Helene Dorn and Hettie Jones* [2016]). In that sense, Carden's book is witness to an ongoing life/afterlife, acknowledging that its own existence will affect the fortunes of its subjects. The writers are all at this point fully aware of their own historicity, and thus many of the "pre-texts" and intertexualities through which their work is now filtered—including this volume—overdetermine their ongoing autobiographical reflections. I wonder if this phenomenon is particular to these women writers of the Beat era, or if it would be true of any relatively marginalized writer who lives to see their day in the sun.

—Maria Damon, Pratt Institute of Art

Works Cited

Friedman, Susan Stanford. "Women's Autobiographical Selves." *The Private Self: Theory and Practice of Women's Autobiographical Writings*, edited by Shari Benstock, U of North Carolina P, 1988, pp. 34-62.

Grace, Nancy M. and Ronna C. Johnson. *Breaking the Rule of Cool: Interviewing and Reading Women Beat Writers*. UP of Mississippi, 2004.

Johnson, Ronna C. and Nancy M. Grace, editors. *Girls Who Wore Black: Women Writing the Beat Generation*. Rutgers UP, 2002.

Kerouac, Jack. "Beatific: Origins of the Beat Generation." *The Portable Jack Kerouac*, edited by Ann Charters, Viking, 1995, pp. 565-73.

Russo, Linda. "Dealing in Parts and Particulars: Joanne Kyger's Early Epic Poetics." *Girls Who Wore Black: Women Writing the Beat Generation*, edited by Ronna C. Johnson and Nancy M. Grace, Rutgers UP, 2002, pp. 178-204.

---. "The Limited Scope of the Recuperative Model: A Context for Reading Joanne Kyger." *Jacket*, vol. 11, 2000, jacketmagazine.com/11/index.shtml.

Kerouac on Record: A Literary Soundtrack
Edited by Simon Warner and Jim Sampas
Bloomsbury Academic, 2018

The Jack Kerouac tribute recording, *Kicks Joy Darkness* (Rykodisc, 1997), demonstrates the sincere affection in which Kerouac is held by the contributing artists—among them Joe Strummer, John Cale, Thurston Moore, Lydia Lunch, Steven Tyler, Patti Smith, Eric Andersen, and many others, a variety that demonstrates Kerouac's reach across musical genres: jazz, folk, punk, indie rock, film instrumentals. This multiplicity is elaborated in *Kerouac on Record* (Bloomsbury 2018), which does a superb job of exploring Kerouac's influence on musicians in its many forms. Combining academic articles, discographies, and interviews with key figures—including Jim Sampas; David Amram, who composed the music for the 1959 film *Pull My Daisy*; "the first *real* rock-crit" Richard Meltzer (151); and Allen Ginsberg—Simon Warner and Jim Sampas's sprawling volume represents the most comprehensive exploration so far of Kerouac's engagements with, and continuing influence on, popular music forms. Beginning with essays and interviews devoted to Kerouac's love of bop jazz, the book moves on to examine the soundtracks to Kerouac's LPs of poetry and the movie adaptation of *The Subterraneans* (1960), before opening out into discussions of Kerouac's influence on artists including Bob Dylan, the Grateful Dead, Van Morrison, Joni Mitchell, Tom Waits, and Patti Smith.

It is a book full of satisfying and surprising revelations. For example, in his essay, "Hit the Road, Jack: Van Morrison and *On the Road*," Peter Mills moves far beyond a simple biographical reading of Kerouac's role in Van Morrison's work. Identifying key stages in Van Morrison's long career, Mills pays close attention to his songs as both written and delivered on record and on stage. Mills demonstrates that lyrical imagery consciously borrowed from Kerouac is only one aspect; of equal importance are the idiosyncratic expressive dynamics of performance, which Mills does a convincing job of showing Van Morrison learned from jazz, blues, and Beat writers. What really counts is "responsiveness to and inhabitation of the immediate, 'lived' moment" (215). Ultimately, Kerouac is but one of many literary influences freely referenced in Van Morrison's work, which evinces "a kind of creative generosity," a desire to share inspiration with listeners (214). Elsewhere, Ronna C. Johnson offers a sophisticated contribution on Kerouac and Patti Smith, suggesting that the former's influence on the latter is evident through "inferential argument and historical context" (289), and seeing Smith's free-form punk experimentations as lying on a continuum with the Beats. Among many enlightening details, the possibility that Kerouac and Smith "both use actual sexual stimulation for a composition aid" stands out (307).

Other contributions to this volume succeed because they locate Beat influence in unexpected places and genres. These include Holly George-Warren's fascinating essay on Kerouac's reception among musicians and other artists—including a young Janis Joplin—in conservative regions of Texas; Matt Theado's essay titled "Kerouac and Country Music," which acknowledges that "[c]ountry music is not a genre that comes immediately to mind when one reads Jack Kerouac's work, nor is it a genre that seemed to appeal to him" (249), shows that the related concerns of home and mythological travel in Kerouac's writing, as well as the nostalgia and yearning for authenticity that frequently color it, share much with country music; and James Sullivan's exploration of Kerouac's importance to punk and new wave practitioners such as Willie Alexander and Richard Hell. Sullivan's most revealing insight, in fact, pertains to a significant *difference* between the Beat generation and the "Blank Generation" of '70s American punk. Richard Hell and the Voidoids's declaration, "I belong to the Blank Generation" (from their 1977 song "Blank Generation"), appears to speak for an entire generational peer group but differs from the essentially sincere and engaged work of Kerouac in its avowed indifference: Hell sings, "I can take it or leave it each time."

That *Kerouac on Record* has the ability to surprise also has much to do with its form. The combination of scholarly writing and interviews worked to great effect in Simon Warner's previous book, *Text and Drugs and Rock 'n' Roll: The Beats and Rock Culture* (2013), and it does so again here. Not only does it have the potential to increase sales beyond the straitened norms of academic publishing (which surely cannot be a bad thing), but it also allows for internal tensions and counterpoints which serve to enliven debates rather than closing off discussion. A case in point is the section on bop jazz. Kerouac's love of jazz music has become almost axiomatic, and it is a great virtue of this book that it manages to offer something new on the subject. In Chapter 1, Jim Burns provides a fascinating biographical account of Kerouac's evolving engagement with jazz music, interspersed with references to the lightly fictionalizes accounts of his jazz experiences in novels such as *The Subterraneans* (1958) and *Desolation Angels* (1965). Burns's closing idea, that "the best way to read Kerouac is with the music of the particular period he is discussing providing an accompaniment to the rhythms of the prose" (28), is highly suggestive and because of the level of detail in his writing, wholly earned.

Marian Jago's essay, "Duet for Saxophone and Pen," provides a review of previous scholarship on the subject; reprises the familiar Kerouac line that he "want[ed] to be considered a jazz poet / blowing a long blues in an afternoon jam/ session on Sunday" (53); but then, through a combination of historical research and forensic analysis of music and prose, makes a strong claim for the centrality of saxophonist Lee Konitz—less celebrated than Charlie Parker, perhaps, but according to Jago "one of the music's most original and masterful improvisers" (55). Jago is indebted to Tim Hunt, whose 2012 article, "'Blow As Deep As You Want To Blow': Time, Textuality, and Jack Kerouac's Development of Spontaneous Prose," she acknowledges as "the only significant consideration of Konitz's influence" before her own (51; *Journal of Beat Studies*, vol. 1). In Hunt's book, *The Textuality of Soulwork*

(2014), developed from that earlier article (and to which Jago, unfortunately, does not refer), Hunt cites at length Kerouac's journal entry for October 8, 1951, in which he expounds on the importance of hearing Lee Konitz play "I'll Remember April." According to Hunt, "Kerouac finds in Konitz's 'I'll Remember April' a validation of writing as process and performance and an alternative to writing solipsistically for one's self" (113).

Jago's impressive knowledge is revealed in her close attention to stylistic features such as Konitz's "trademark use of extended eight-note lines marked by an unorthodox use of accents and poly-rhythmic effects" (53). Following this article is an interview with Konitz, conducted by Jago herself, in which the saxophonist initially dismisses Beat writers as guys "just trying to make effects" and "showing off" (74, 75), and then, through Jago's patient line of questioning, warms to the idea that Kerouac was a genuine fan of his work, finally thanking his interviewer for her renewed insights. As well as providing one of the book's more affecting moments, it serves as a necessary reminder of the disjunction that might exist between scholarship and its objects, and yet of the important connecting functions scholarship can have.

The scope and ambition of *Kerouac on Record* cannot be faulted, and the energy produced by the multi-disciplinary contributions is compelling. This, in fact, is the volume's greatest strength. It insists on viewing Beat creativity, exemplified here by Kerouac, as interdisciplinary from the very beginning, and thus insists on a model of cultural analysis that takes its cue from that interdisciplinary, expansive, inclusive outlook. Kerouac, as revealed through these essays and interviews, was not just a writer who liked jazz; he was an artist intent on exploring and experimenting with hybrid sensory forms that brought music, prose, and concrete visual perception into harmony. He was also, as many of the contributors claim, an accomplished improviser and performer. Likewise, the artists who drew on Kerouac as inspiration, even those who simply name-checked his stories and characters in their songs, might be seen as musicians with a literary sensibility, rather than simply musicians who had read certain poems and novels with a high degree of cultural capital. Appendix V, "Jack and Neal on Record," a listing by Dave Moore and Horst Spandler of recordings that relate to Kerouac and/or Cassady, shows just how many of these artists there have been.

It should be noted that the appendices are wonderful resources in themselves. They include two important essays by Kerouac—"Essentials of Spontaneous Prose" from 1958, in which the famous line "[b]low as deep as you want" can be found, and "Belief and Technique for Modern Prose," published in 1959—as well as an expertly annotated discography of Kerouac's recorded works and a discography of tribute albums. As noted above, Appendix V, "Jack and Neal on Record," is a valuable resource for researchers. Running to 24 pages, it constitutes an impressive piece of scholarship and demonstrates almost as effectively as the essays and interviews preceding it how profoundly and widely felt Kerouac's cultural legacy has been.

Kerouac on Record is not perfect. An accusation one might level at *Text and Drugs and Rock 'n' Roll* is also relevant in this case: that the quest for wide coverage, driven by a no doubt sincere belief in Kerouac's influence, results in some less persuasive accounts. Nancy M. Grace's innovative essay on Joni Mitchell is a model of how to do it right. She turns the tenuousness of Kerouac and Mitchell's connection into a virtue, proceeding from Mitchell's vehement and stereotyped dismissals of Beat culture, before reflecting on the complex question of influence itself, how it might emerge as much from willful discontinuities and inversions as continuities and explicit borrowings. An essay on Jim Morrison, however, relies on a series of less convincing similarities and coincidences between Kerouac and the Doors's lead singer—the "darker side" they shared (197), partly fuelled in Morrison's case by "a hatred of authority" (198), their sudden fame and their self-destructive tendencies. The evidence for direct influence here feels forced, consisting of some novels likely read, some poetry written, a meeting with the poet Michael McClure. What the author, Jay Jeff Jones, is striving for, it seems, is a *spiritual* resonance between the two artists. The structure of the piece, which cuts between critical incidents in the lives of the two artists, does at least enable a sense of this resonance to emerge.

A more serious weakness of the collection concerns race. References are made throughout—in Warner's introduction, for example, and in Jonah Raskin's essay on Kerouac's spoken-word recordings—to Kerouac's fascination with African American culture, his celebration, in Raskin's words, of "jazz, the blues, bebop and 'The Negro' as 'the essential American'" (83). The contributors who make such (perfectly legitimate) observations nonetheless fail satisfactorily to discuss the problematic aspects of this fascination: the risk of reducing the figure of the African American to a set of desired and fetishized essential characteristics—spontaneity, physicality, connection to the earth and "earthy language" (83)—and consequently the appropriation of supposed "negro" sensibilities by white hipsters, as exemplified in Norman Mailer's 1957 essay, "The White Negro." To acknowledge more explicitly the dangers of such views would not cast doubt on the inherent sincerity of Kerouac's interest in predominantly African American forms of artistic expression, but it would enrich the contextual background for this volume by showing the complex interactions of race and politics in the history and reception of the music that was so transformative for him.

Kerouac on Record is nevertheless a significant achievement. For scholars like me who are interested in the interactions between music and literature, or who attempt to apply techniques of literary analysis to musical texts, it is an inspiration. For anyone interested in Beat culture and the work of Jack Kerouac, it is invaluable.

—James Peacock, Keele University, United Kingdom

Mountains, Rivers, and the Great Earth:
Reading Gary Snyder and Dōgen in an Age of Ecological Crisis
Jason M. Wirth
State University of New York Press, 2017

Mountains, Rivers, and the Great Earth by Jason M. Wirth, professor of philosophy at Seattle University, appears in the SUNY series "Environmental Philosophy and Ethics." Wirth has previously written about wilderness and nature in the work of Friedrich Wilhelm Joseph Schelling (1775-1854) and Maurice Merleau-Ponty (1908-1961). Wirth's 2015 study, *Schelling's Practice of the Wild: Time, Art, Imagination*, stages an imagined dialogue between the Romantic German philosopher Schelling and postwar American poet/essayist Gary Snyder, asserting that Schelling, like Snyder, calls for a "practice of the wild" (22). In the book under review, Wirth meditates on Snyder's words about and verbal manifestations of wilderness in relation to the philosophical and spiritual implications of "the Great Earth," as signified by the writings of Eihei Dōgen (1200-1253). The book explores connections among a family of related concepts (e.g., the Dao, the Wild, the Great Earth, and nonduality) against the background of the current ecological crisis (e.g., rising ocean temperatures, rampant development, and the oncoming Sixth Extinction) to espouse the idea that opening our minds in the manner of Dōgen and Snyder's writings is conducive to the kind of "earth democracy" that Earth as a biological system sorely needs.

Snyder's references to Dōgen appear with increasing frequency in his writing after influential translations began to appear in the 1980s, especially *The Moon in a Dewdrop*, edited by Kazuaki Tanahashi. Wirth does not merely gloss Snyder's Dōgen references; he reads Snyder and Dōgen contrapuntally, developing connections between ecological and philosophical/religious implications within the texts. The most striking aspect of Wirth's book is that it does not propose to "chart the development of [Dōgen and Snyder's] respective ideas or to elaborate every facet of their thinking and writing," but instead offers a "meditation and philosophical engagement that seeks to read, think, and practice *along with* both of them in a manner that is mindful of the place from where one reads them today," seeking "to express something *of the place from which* Snyder and Dōgen practice, think, and write" (xiii). In marking a distance between his own writing and conventional academic criticism, Wirth is "forswearing the traditional academic distance that confuses the rigor of careful thought with the spirit of abstraction and the academic professionalism that keeps issues at hand at a safe distance" (xxiii). While I strongly object to the implication that Snyder criticism has been otherworldly or overly filled with jargon—this simply is not the case—the experiment that Wirth initiates is an interesting one. Working in between literary, religious, and philosophical texts, he attempts not to *describe* textbook definitions of Buddhist dependent co-arising or nonduality, but rather to work out a form of commentary that proceeds from such a mindset. The book is a hybrid in which the text wanders between literary criticism and philosophical commentary, on the one hand, and the encouraging words of a mindful preacher on the other.

The general idea that Wirth meditates upon is the Buddhist concept of *pratītyasamutpāda* as it applies to ecology; that is, how humans relate to the earth. In English, this concept is generally translated as "dependent co-arising" and denotes the idea that permanent, unchanging identities do not exist because all phenomena are radically contingent. When Dōgen said that mountains walk just as a person walks, he was proposing a riddle with various solutions. The stillness of mountains is not apart from a person's walking; also, mountains appear still because our views of them are human sized—within the scale of a human life time we do not perceive that mountains zoom up from the bottom of the ocean or get worn down over time. In a developed discussion of Dōgen's important essay "Time Being," a meditation on nonduality and temporality, Wirth solves the riddle in this way: "If the mountain is not a fixed point of reference for time [...] time marks the emptiness of the form of the mountain (that a mountain is not first itself and then endures through time). Rather than a continuity through, the mountain is time as discontinuity, as difference" (13). In other words, things that look solid and unchanging are processes, but all processes are made up of present moments. Mountains often appear as iconic representations of stability, but Dōgen, Snyder, and Wirth commune in the fluidity of mountains.

The book is rather short—116 pages, not including endnotes—and is composed of six chapters in three two-chapter sections. The three sections are "The Great Earth," "Turtle Island," and "Earth Democracy." The imagistic/thematic focus is clear, but the argument—Wirth calls it a meditation or a practice rather than an academic argument—is sometimes less clear. Wirth suggests that if, through our practice, we realized properly how we exist, we would not see "the Great Earth," "the Wild," or "Turtle Island" as other than ourselves, and if we saw that we *are* the Great Earth, we would not be facing catastrophic climate change. Wirth presents Snyder's poetry and prose as models for proper appreciation of the world as it is, as opposed to the assemblage of resources we are trained to imagine in its place. The second chapter, "Geology (Poetic Word)," works out connections to the scroll tradition and the "painted rice cake" metaphor that Snyder introduces in an epigraph to *Mountains and Rivers Without End* (1996) about how we *are* satisfied by a painted rice cake. This chapter also contains connections to modernist artist Paul Klee and Kyoto School philosopher Nishitani Keiji, and discussions of *The Lotus Sutra*. Bits and pieces of Snyder's work accompany these riffs, and the chapter ends with the line "[m]ay all beings flourish" (53). Readers may agree with this general wish, but Wirth's Zen *teisho* (sermonic commentary given to a practicing community) might lose some readers who would prefer a tighter focus. As the book is a SUNY publication rather than a book from Shambhala or Wisdom Publications, the blurring of the line between academic utterance and confessional assertion can be irritating. "May all beings flourish" is a noble sentiment and a strong practice, but I feel uncomfortable reading them in a book like this. I would feel the same way if I read an essay about Mary

Karr or another Christian writer that ended with "[m]ay Christ be with you." The best parts are those in which Wirth closely examines a tradition (the Mountains and Water painting school) or concept (being time). These parts will be of great interest to Snyder scholars and perhaps other Beat generation scholars who are interested in Buddhism, although there is only brief mention of writers such as Allen Ginsberg and Philip Whalen in the book.

The next two chapters are "Place (Land and Sea, Earth and Sky)" and "Bears (The Many Palaces of the Earth)." These chapters are largely about sense of place and the nonduality of humans and animals, two especially important topics in Snyder's writing. They each include an excursus about other American writers, in the first instance, Herman Melville, and in the second, William Faulkner. The discussion of *Moby-Dick* and place in "Place" seems out of place. The connections that Wirth seeks to establish between Melville and Snyder are not especially clear. While it is true that *Moby-Dick* shows Melville to be an early critic of American imperialism, the discussion of Melville's sense of place feels like a step down from Snyder's writing on place. This section's obtrusion seems as if a conference paper had been folded into the text. The discussion of Faulkner's "The Bear" is also semi-detached, but the thematic match is much more convincing. Wirth does not mention this interesting detail: Snyder had students read Faulkner's novella "The Bear" in his "Literature and Wilderness" class when he started teaching at University of California-Davis in the mid-1980s. Wirth's discussion of "The Bear" relates to Snyder's writings about place and wilderness quite well.

The third section includes "The Great Potlach" and "Seeds of Earth Democracy." Wirth opens discussion of the potlach concept—a social ritual in which people increase their honor by giving gifts to others, as opposed to increasing their status by accumulating possessions—by discussing the Tārā poem in *Mountains and Rivers Without End*. Tārā is a female Tibetan *yidam*, meaning a deity upon whom one meditates to generate qualities such as compassion associated with that deity. She is depicted as beautiful and vibrant—she is sitting but has her left leg out, as she is getting up from the seated position in order to save sentient beings. While *Mountains, Rivers, and the Great Earth* refers more frequently to Dōgen's Zen Buddhist texts, the poem "An Offering for Tārā" recounts a puja (ritual offering) to Tārā, the goddess of compassion. The poem briefly weaves in sexual imagery associated with the Vajrayana or Tantric path in Buddhism, and as I have argued in "The Sexual Politics of Divine Femininity: Tārā in Transition in Gary Snyder's Poetry," Tārā is used to signify a broad feminine principle in Snyder's writing. She is a personification of compassion matching the duality-severing sword of a Vajrayana deity, Manjushri. The puja of Snyder's poem, Wirth argues, symbolizes not the gift-exchange that we *might* enjoy with nature, but rather the one that we *do* participate in, whether or not we acknowledge it. The final chapter, "Seeds of Earth Democracy," connects ideas about the commons (i.e., lands and resources that are not owned by individuals or corporations but which instead are available for shared use by members of the community) that Snyder deploys in *Practice of the Wild* (1990) with Shiva Vandana's concept of "Earth Democracy" as a method of achieving ecological justice. Buddhist practices such as an ethical insistence on *ahimsā* (non-harming) are, Wirth admits, only partial solutions to attaining ecological justice, but he asserts this value is an essential part.

The book only touches in passing on Snyder's relationship with writers of the Beat generation and with countercultural thought, but it is a useful volume for those who want to better understand the logic of what we might call Zen expression. Those completely unfamiliar with the concept of nonduality should begin by reading the early chapters of David Loy's *Nonduality: A Study in Comparative Philosophy* (1988), which describes the matter in a more linear way. Wirth's book will also be of interest to environmental humanities scholars who are interested in considering non-Western approaches to such matters.

—John Whalen-Bridge, National University of Singapore

Works Cited

Dōgen, Eihei. *Moon in a Dewdrop: Writings of Zen Master Dōgen*. Edited by Kazuaki Tanahashi. North Point Press, 1985.

Loy, David. *Nonduality: A Study in Comparative Philosophy*. Yale UP, 1988.

Shiva, Vandana. *Earth Democracy: Justice, Sustainability and Peace*. Zed Books, 2005.

Snyder, Gary. *Mountains and Rivers Without End*. Counterpoint, 1996.

Whalen-Bridge, John. "The Sexual Politics of Divine Femininity: Tārā in Transition in Gary Snyder's Poetry." *Partial Answers*, vol. 5, no. 2, 2007, pp. 219-44.

Wirth, Jason M. *Schelling's Practice of the Wild: Time, Art, Imagination*. SUNY P, 2015.

The Beat Index 2018

The Beat Index provides a chronicle of recent scholarship, including dissertations, in the field of Beat studies. The artists and other Beat generation figures represented here are core to the movement or are associated with then-contemporary and complementary avant-garde literary movements. Abstracts are included when available; these are publisher or author abstracts and may appear in excerpted form. Texts are organized alphabetically according to Beat or Beat-associated author. If we have omitted a title, such omission was unintentional, and we will appreciate being informed of the omission so we can include it in the next volume of the journal.

The Beat Generation

Garton-Gundling, Kyle. *Enlightened Individualism: Buddhism and Hinduism in American Literature from the Beats to the Present*. The Ohio State UP, 2019.

> This book addresses how post-1945 American writers, including Kerouac, Alice Walker, and Maxine Hong Kingston, explored what Buddhist and Hindu influences offer American identities. "Enlightened individualism" uses Buddhist and Hindu philosophy to reframe American freedom in terms of spiritual liberation, and it reinterprets Asian teachings through Western traditions of political activism and countercultural provocation. Garton-Gundling argues that although works by Kerouac, Walker, Kingston, and others wrestle with issues of exoticism and appropriation, their characters are meaningfully challenged and changed by Asian faiths.

Lane, Véronique, editor. *French and Beat Literatures: A History of Mutual Appropriation, Reception, and Translation*, special issue of *L'esprit createur: The International Quarterly of French and Francophone Studies*, vol. 58, no. 4, 2018.

> This special issue attends to neglected as well as major Beat writers and opens a dialogue between Anglophone and Francophone scholarship. One of its main aims is to inspire further archival and textual work by giving new weight to the crucial yet problematic role of publishers, editors, and translators to convey French and Beat literatures across and between languages and cultures. Contents include the following:
>
> Bellarsi, Franca. "Jean Cocteau et le sang poétique de la Beat Generation."

Kerouac's *Doctor Sax* and many of Ginsberg's poems are analyzed in light of the cocthalean aesthetics of waking dream. (Essay in French.)

Earle, Jason. "American Schizo: William Burroughs and Semiotext(e)."

Earle analyzes the role of Burroughs within the theoretical, aesthetic, and political project of New York-based journal *Semiotext(e)*. It demonstrates how *Semiotext(e)* fashioned an image of Burroughs as theorist by choosing to foreground his politics, sexuality, and radical philosophy; and how Burroughs served as a crucial link between the American counterculture and post-1968 French thought.

Harris, Oliver. "William Burroughs' Cut-Ups Lost and Found in Translation."

Harris argues that what has been lost in translation for Francophone readers can make visible key features of cut-up texts that have been missed or misunderstood by anglophone readers, above all their intertextuality.

Horton, James. "Mary Beach and Claude Pélieu's Translations and Adaptations of Allen Ginsberg's Work."

This article explores how the perception of Beat writers in France was influenced by the translations produced from the mid-1960s to the mid-1970s by Mary Beach and Claude Pélieu with a close textual reading of their 1967 version of Ginsberg's "Kaddish."

Hussey, Andrew. "From Bucharest to the Beat Hotel: Isidore Isou and the Lettrist Revolution on the Left Bank."

The aim of this article is to reinstate Isidore Isou as a twentieth century avant-gardist by considering his practice. The article focuses on the parallels between *lettriste* word collages and the "cut-ups" of William S. Burroughs.

Lane, Véronique. "Introduction: Materializing the 'Eternal French Connexion.'"

---. "Tristan Corbiere's *Amours jaunes* in Allen Ginsberg's Early Poetry."

From the 1950s to the 1980s, Ginsberg inscribed Tristan Corbière's poetry in his own, and in ways that concealed as much as they revealed. Working backwards from Ginsberg's allusion to Corbière in the 1986 variorum edition of "Howl," this article offers the first intertextual reading of their poetry.

Melehy, Hassan. "Godard Gets the Blues: Movies, Music, and Baraka."

> Melehy addresses Jean-Luc Godard's quotations from Amiri Baraka (LeRoi Jones) in two movies. In *Masculin féminin* (1966), Godard stages a scene from Baraka's 1964 racially charged play *Dutchman*. In *One Plus One* (aka *Sympathy for the Devil*) (1968), Godard's Rolling Stones documentary, an actor reads from Baraka's writings on the relationship of rock and roll to black music.

Peno-Lacassagne, Oliver. "La Beat Generation en France: Avant-garde vs Underground."

> The French reception of the Beat generation is mixed. First readings, whether interested or enthusiastic, in the early 1960s came from Maoist-focused *Tel Quel*. In contrast, the emerging alternative press (in particular, the newspaper *Actuel*) published the major texts of the American counterculture. (Essay in French.)

Pinette, Susan. "Jack Kerouac's French, American, and Quebecois Receptions: From Deterritorialization to Reterritorialization."

> This article explores the statements Deleuze made about Kerouac's works to clarify the paradox underlying Deleuze's reading of Kerouac and how this exemplifies Kerouac's reception in France and Quebec.

Van Gageldonk, Maarten. "The Representation of Literary and Cultural Paris in *Olympia Review* (1961-1963)."

> Between 1961 and 1963, Maurice Girodias's Olympia Press published four issues of *Olympia Magazine*, an English-language magazine published from Paris. This article argues that *Olympia Magazine*, largely unstudied so far, was representative of Girodias's unique reconceptualization of Paris for an anglophone and largely foreign readership.

Lee, A. Robert, editor. *The Routledge Handbook of International Beat Literature.* Routledge, 2019.

> This collection presents Beat voices from across the Americas of Canada and Mexico, the Anglophone world of England, Scotland or Australia, the Europe of France or Italy and from the Mediterranean of Greece and the Maghreb, and from Scandinavia and Russia, together with the Asia of Japan and China. This anthology maps relevant kinds of Beat voices, names, and

texts. The scope is hemispheric, Atlantic and Pacific, West and East. It recognizes the Beat inscribed in languages other than English and reflective of different cultural histories. The majority of contributors come from origins or affiliations beyond the United States, whether in a different English or languages spanning Spanish, Danish, Turkish, Greek, or Chinese. Contents include the following:

Antonic, Thomas. "Beat Authorship and Beat Influences in Austrian Literature."

Bellarsi, Franca. "Transmuting Beat Energies in the Belgian Francophone Matrix: Maelström ReEvolution or the Brussels Reincarnation of the Beat Spirit."

Birns, Nicholas. "Beat Australia: Hydra to Balmain."

Encarnacio-Pinedo, Estibaliz. "Beat Affinities in Spanish Poetry."

Epstein, Thomas. "Russian Beat: Wilderness of Mirrors."

Escobar de la Garma, Alberto. "The Beat Presence in Mexican Literature."

Forsgren, Frida. "Norwegian Beat Culture: Reading Beat and Being Beat in Oslo in the 1950s."

Greiffenstern, Alexander. "German Beats: Friendship and Collaboration."

Heal, Benjamin J. "The Beats on China and Chinese 'Beats': Cross Cultural Influences, Impact and Legacy."

Lee, A. Robert. "Introduction."

---. "Beat Japan: Shiraishi's Jazz Scroll and Sakaki's Foot Trail."

Louai, El Habib. "Moroccan Beat Writers: Mrabet, Choukri, Layachi."

Mackay, Polina. "The Beat Generation and Contemporary Greek Poetry."

Mortenson, Erik. "Beat Turkey: A Belated Influence."

Movin, Lars. "Denmark's To Beat or Not to Beat: Turèll, Ulrich, Laugesen."

Ost, Lisa Avdic. "Swedish Beat: Sture Darlstöm, Ulf Lundrell and the Influence of the Beat Generation on Modern Swedish Literature."

Pacini, Peggy. "Êtes-Vous Beat? Contemporary French Beat Writing."

Paton, Fiona. "Cosmopolitan Scum: A Genealogy of Beat in Subaltern Scottish Literature."

Pietrasz, Andrzej and Tomasz Sawczuk. "Activists and Stuntmen: Envisioning Polish Beat."

Stefanelli, Maria Anita. "Children of Anarchy: Shoulder to Shoulder with the Italian Beats."

Streip, Katharine. "Canada Beats: A Complex Legacy."

Van der Bent, Jaap. "Beat Influences in Dutch and Flemish Literature."

Veivo, Harri. "Beat Poetry in Finland in the 1950s."

Walker, Luke. "Beat Britain: Poetic Vision and Division in Albion's 'Underground.'"

Melehy, Hassan. *Beat Generation Writers as Readers of World Literature*, special issue of *Humanities*, 2018-2019, www.mdpi.com/journal/humanities/special_issues/Beat_Generation.

> This special issue of *Humanities* seeks to explore the ways that Beat generation writers read world literature and incorporated what they learned from it in their own writing. Note: Essays are posted online as they are finalized, so additional essays in this volume may be published at a later date. Contents include the following:

Belletto, Steven. "The Beat Generation Meets the Hungry Generation: U.S.-Calcutta Networks and the 1960s 'Revolt of the Personal.'"

> The essay emphasizes the close relationship between aesthetics and politics in Hungry Generation writing and suggests that Ginsberg's mid-1960s turn to political activism is reminiscent of strategies employed by Hungry Generation writers.

Encarnación-Pinedo, Estíbaliz. "Intertextuality in Diane di Prima's *Loba*: Religious Discourse and Feminism."

> This essay explores di Prima's particular use of world narratives in her long poem *Loba* through Eve, the Virgin Mary, and Lilith, three of the many female characters whose textual representations are challenged in *Loba*.

Nelson, Paul E. "Projective Verse: The Spiritual Legacy of the Beat Generation."

>This essay posits that it is Michael McClure's use of Projective Verse that future generations of writers and readers will come to appreciate as that movement's spiritual legacy.

Nourmand, Tony and Michael Shulman, editors. *The Beat Scene: Photographs by Burt Glinn*. Reel Art Press, 2018.

>This volume features a collection of largely unseen photographs of the Beat generation by Magnum photographer Burt Glinn. The images were discovered when Reel Art Press was working with Glinn's widow, Elena, on a larger retrospective of Glinn's work. Archived with the negatives was a short essay by Jack Kerouac titled "And This Is The Beat Nightlife of New York," which is published here alongside the photographs. The book features black-and-white shots, and also—unusual, for images of this era—more than 70 in color. The photographs were shot between 1957 and 1960 in New York and San Francisco and feature nearly everyone involved in the scene, including writers and artists such as Ginsberg, Kerouac, Corso, Ferlinghetti, LeRoi Jones, Jay DeFeo, Wally Hedrick, and many more.

Stephenson, Gregory. *Points of Intersection: Meeting Paul Bowles, Allen Ginsberg, Brion Gysin, Robert Graves, Pauline Réage, and Others*. EyeCorner Press, 2018.

>This book explores encounters with significant literary figures, including conversations with Paul Bowles, Mohammed Mrabet, Brion Gysin, Pauline Réage, Robert Graves, Maurice Girodias, Berthe Cleyrergue, Edouard Roditi, Ginsberg, and Peter Orlovsky.

Tietchen, Todd F. *Technomodern Poetics: The American Literary Avant-Garde at the Start of the Information Age*. UP of Iowa, 2018.

>This book examines how some of the best-known writers of the era described the tensions between technical, literary, and media cultures at the dawn of the Digital Age. Allen Ginsberg, Charles Olson, Jack Kerouac, and Frank O'Hara, among others, anthologized in Donald Allen's iconic *The New American Poetry: 1945–1960* provided a canon of work increasingly relevant to our technological present.

Amiri Baraka

Calihman, Matthew and Gerald Early. *Approaches to Teaching Baraka's* Dutchman. Modern Language Association of America, 2018.

>This book is a guide to teaching *Dutchman*, the most widely studied work of the writer-activist Amiri Baraka (1934-2014). In addition to the pedagogically focused essays listed below, the volume contains materials on biography, autobiography, book-length studies, edited collections, special issues, early productions, editions, and the following essays:
>
>Ade, Andrew. "Teaching *Dutchman* through Creative Writing."
>
>Bloom, James, D. "Amiri Baraka and Philip Roth: Passing, Place, and Identity."
>
>Calihman, Matthew. "*Dutchman* as Black Avant-Garde Historial Drama."
>
>Chakkalakal, Tess. "*Dutchman's* Uncle Tom."
>
>Cocola, Jim. "*Dutchman* in the Round."
>
>Corkery, Caleb. "Teaching *Dutchman* with Chappelle's Show: Arguments along the Color Line."
>
>Hemmer, Kurt. "Breaking from the Beats: Teaching *Dutchman* as a Critique of Bohemianism."
>
>Hiro, Molly. "'No Metaphors,' 'No Grunts': *Dutchman*, Black Art, and Authenticity."
>
>Hoey, Danny M. "*Dutchman*, the Black Body, and the Law."
>
>Jakubiak, Katarzyna. "Teaching *Dutchman* from an International Perspective."
>
>Marcoux, Jean-Philippe. "*Dutchman* and Black Vernacular Culture."
>
>McBride, William Thomas. "*Dutchman* Heaped in Modern Cinema."
>
>Miller, D. Quentin. "'And That's How the Blues Was Born': Baraka's *Dutchman* and Baldwin's *Blues for Mister Charlie* in Conversation."
>
>Mitchell, Koritha. "What's Love Got to Do with It? Everything! Teaching *Dutchman* and 'The Revolutionary Theatre.'"

Mix, Deborah M. "Culture and Violence in *Dutchman* and the Black Arts Movement."

Morris, Daniel. "Baraka's Aesthetic Radicalism: *Dutchman*'s Modernist Root."

Ponnuswami, Meenakshi, "*Dutchman* in the Drama Class."

Sargent, Andrew. "'Free of Your Own History': Implicating Students in *Dutchman*."

Schur, Richard. "Reading *Dutchman*'s Setting."

Williams, Roland Leander, Jr. "*Dutchman*, *A Raisin' in the Sun*, and the History of Minstrel Theater."

Dumitru, Teodara. "Gaming the World-System: Creativity, Politics, and Beat Influence in the Poetry of the 1980s Generation." *Romanian Literature as World Literature*. Edited by Mircea Martin, Christian Moraru, and Andrei Terian, Bloomsbury Academic, 2018.

Grundy, David. *A Black Arts Poetry Machine: Amiri Baraka and the Umbra Poets*. Bloomsbury, 2019.

> This book brings together new archival research and detailed close readings of poetry by Amiri Baraka, Lorenzo Thomas, Calvin Hernton, and others. Considering how their innovative poetic forms engaged with radical political responses to state violence and urban insurrection, the book highlights the continuing relevance of the work of the Umbra Workshop and is essential reading for anyone interested in 20th-century American poetry.

Melehy, Hassan. "Godard Gets the Blues: Movies, Music, and Baraka." *L'esprit créateur*, vol. 58, no. 4, 2018, pp. 149-167. See Lane entry under Beat Generation.

William S. Burroughs

Hawkins, Joan and Alex Wermer-Colan, editors. *William S. Burroughs: Cutting Up the Century*, Indiana UP, 2019.

> This anthology focuses on Burroughs's overarching cut-up project and its relevance to the American twentieth century. *The Nova Trilogy* (*The Soft*

Machine, *Nova Express*, and *The Ticket That Exploded*) remains the best known of his textual cut-up creations, but he searched out multimedia for use in works of collage. This collection includes previously unpublished cut-up work by Burroughs, such as cut-ups of critical responses to his own work, collages on the Vietnam War and the Watergate scandal, excerpts from his dream journals, and rare diary entries Burroughs wrote about his wife, Joan. It also features original essays, interviews, and discussions by established Burroughs scholars. The volume contains:

Douglas, Ann, Anne Waldman, and Regina Weinreich. "Gender Trouble: A Critical Roundtable on Burroughs and Gender."

Galvin, Kristen. "The Nova Convention: Celebrating the Burroughs of Downtown New York."

Gray, Kathelin. "Burroughs and the Biosphere, 1974-1997."

Harris, Oliver. "Burroughs and Biography: An Interview with Barry Miles."

---. "Cutting Up the Century."

Hemmer, Kurt. "Queer Outlaws Losing: The Betrayal of the Outlaw Underground in *The Place of Dead Roads*."

Hibbard, Alan. "William S. Burroughs' Spirit of Collaboration."

Lane, Véronique. "Rimbaud and Genet, Burroughs' Favorite Mirrors."

Murphy, Timothy S. "Interference Zones: William Burroughs in the Interstices of Globalization."

Nyerges, Aaron. "Beat Regionalism: Burroughs in Mexico, Burroughs in Women's Studies."

Palmer, Landon. "The Disembodied Fry: William S. Burroughs and Vocal Performance."

Sandweiss, Eric. "Cut-Up City: William S. Burroughs' 'St. Louis Return.'"

Schneiderman, Davis and Oliver Harris. "Cross the Wounded Galaxies: A Conversation about the Cut-Up Trilogy."

Streip, Katharine. "William S. Burroughs, Transcendence Porn, and *The Ticket That Exploded*."

> Stricklin, Blake. "'Word Falling...Photo Falling': William S. Burroughs and the Word as Written Image."
>
> Vasquez, Joshua. "*Naked Lunch* and the Art of Incompleteness: The Use of Genre in Burroughs' Book and Cronenberg's Film."
>
> Waldman, Anne. "The Burroughs Effect."
>
> Weidner, Cha. "Mutable Forms: The Proto-Ecology of William Burroughs' Early Cut-Ups."
>
> Wermer-Colan, Alex. "William S. Burroughs' Imperial Decadence: Subversive Literature in the Cynical Age of the American Century."
>
> Wermer-Colan, Alex and Joan Hawkins. "Introduction: Cutting Up the Century."

Rae, Casey. *William S. Burroughs and the Cult of Rock 'n' Roll*, U of Texas P, 2019.

> This book reveals the transformations in music history that can be traced to Burroughs. Rae brings to life Burroughs's parallel rise to fame among daring musicians of the 1960s, '70s, and '80s, when it became a rite of passage to hang out with the author or to experiment with his cut-up techniques for producing revolutionary lyrics (as did the Beatles and Radiohead). Notable discussions include Burroughs exploring the occult with David Bowie, providing Lou Reed with gritty depictions of street life, and counseling Patti Smith about coping with fame.

Taylor, Steven, editor. *Don't Hide the Madness: William S. Burroughs in Conversation with Allen Ginsberg*. Three Room Press, 2018.

> Ginsberg and Burroughs discuss literary influences and personal history in a never-before-published three-day conversation following the release of the David Cronenberg film of Burroughs's classic novel *Naked Lunch*. The visit coincided with the shamanic exorcism of the demon that Burroughs believed had caused him to fatally shoot his common law wife, Joan Vollmer Burroughs, in 1951—the event that Burroughs believed had driven his work as a writer. The conversation is interspersed with photographs by Ginsberg revealing Burroughs's daily activities from his painting studio to the shooting range.

Thomas, Joseph T., Jr. "Street Families and Wild Boys: A Collage for William S. Burroughs." *Pacific Coast Philology,* vol. 53, no. 2, 2018.

This article uses Burroughs's novel *The Wild Boy: A Book of the Dead* as a mechanism for understanding contemporary constructions of the child. Placing Burroughs's novel in conversation with Lee Edelman's *No Future: Queer Theory and the Death Drive*, Thomas explores how Burroughs's conception of the child offers a provocatively powerful alternative to Edelman's "Child," the latter lashed forever to "reproductive futurity," whereas the former radically resists the conservative, homophobic status quo it serves to perpetuate.

Gregory Corso

Dar, Sarah. "Conclusion: 'Know that the earth will madonna the Bomb.'" *Writing Nature in Cold War American Literature,* Edinburgh UP, 2018, pp. 205-211.

The conclusion to this book focuses on Corso's 1958 concrete poem "Bomb."

Diane di Prima

Calonne, David Stephen. *Diane di Prima: Visionary Poetics and the Hidden Religions,* Bloomsbury, 2019.

Calonne charts the life work of di Prima through close readings of her poetry, prose, and autobiographical writings, exploring her thorough immersion in world spiritual traditions and how these studies informed both the form and content of her *oeuvre*. Di Prima's engagement in what she calls "the hidden religions" includes her years at Swarthmore College and in New York City; her move to San Francisco and immersion in Zen; her mid-sixties researches into the *I Ching*, Paracelsus, John Dee, Heinrich Cornelius Agrippa, alchemy, Tarot, and Kabbalah; and her later interest in Tibetan Buddhism.

Encarnación-Pinedo, Estibaliz. "Intertextuality in Diane di Prima's *Loba*: Religious Discourse and Feminism." See Melehy entry under Beat Generation.

Orsini, Maximillian. *The Buddhist Beat Poetics of Diane di Prima and Lenore Kandel*. Beatdom Books. 2018.

Orsini examines the impact of two female poets, di Prima and Kandel, in shaping American Buddhist poetics. Orsini charts the evolution of their poetry against a backdrop of cultural conservatism and explores how their journeys differed from those of their male counterparts.

Robert Duncan

Katz, Daniel. "Robert Duncan and the 1960s: Psychoanalysis, Politics, Kitsch." *Qui Parle*, vol. 27, no. 1, 2018.

Bob Dylan

Walker, Luke. "'Tangled Up in Blake': The Triangular Relationship Among Dylan, Blake, and the Beats." *Rock and Romanticism: Blake, Wordsworth, and Rock from Dylan to U2*. Edited by James Rovira. Lexington Books, 2018.

> *Rock and Romanticism* is an edited anthology that seeks to explain how rock and roll is a Romantic phenomenon that sheds light, retrospectively, on what literary Romanticism was at its different points of origin and on what it has become in the present.

Lawrence Ferlinghetti

Belletto, Steven. "The Beat Generation Meets the Hungry Generation: U.S.-Calcutta Networks and the 1960s 'Revolt of the Personal.'" See Melehy entry under Beat Generation.

Allen Ginsberg

Belletto, Steven. "The Beat Generation Meets the Hungry Generation: U.S.-Calcutta Networks and the 1960s 'Revolt of the Personal.'" See Melehy entry under Beat Generation.

Dandeles, Gregory. "Avant-Gardes at the Iron Curtain: A Transnational Reading of Allen Ginsberg and the Soviet Estradny Movement." Dissertation Abstracts, 2018.

> This dissertation uncovers how Ginsberg's family connections to Russia, his interest in Russian Futurist and Estradny poetry, his travels to the Soviet Union and other Soviet Bloc countries in 1965, as well as his collaborations and friendships with Russian poets Andrei Voznesensky and Yevgeny Yevtushenko shaped his shift in the late sixties to a new style of aural

composition and excursions into new genres and modes of performance. It argues for the importance of reading across national and linguistic borders to advance our understanding of the cultures both inside and beyond them.

Hollenbach, Lisa. "Broadcasting 'Howl.'" *Modernism/Modernity*, vol. 3, no. 2, 2018.

Morris, Daniel. "Convergence Cultures: Modern and Contemporary Poetry and the Graphic Novel." *The Cambridge History of the Graphic Novel*, edited by Stephen E. Tabachnick. Cambridge UP, 2018.

> This article focuses on Eric Drooker's graphic novel of Ginsberg's "Howl."

Rosenthal, Bob. *Straight Around Allen: The Business of Being Allen Ginsberg*. Beatdom Books, 2018.

> Bob Rosenthal worked as Ginsberg's personal secretary for over two decades. In this intimate book, he discusses what it was like to be behind the scenes of the Allen Ginsberg industry. Rosenthal recounts the highs and lows of employment in the poet's circle, from first encounter to Ginsberg's death.

Taylor, Steven, editor. *Don't Hide the Madness: William S. Burroughs in Conversation with Allen Ginsberg*. Three Room Press, 2018. See entry under Burroughs.

Warnes, Andrew. "The Drive-Thru Supermarket: Shopping Carts and the Foodscapes of American Literature." *Food and Literature*, edited by Gitanjali Shahani, Cambridge UP, 2018.

Lenore Kandel

Orsini, Maximillian. *The Buddhist Beat Poetics of Diane di Prima and Lenore Kandel*. Beatdom Books, 2018. See entry under di Prima.

Jack Kerouac

Bandera, Sandrina, Allesandro Castiglioni, and Emma Zanella, editors. *Kerouac: Beat Painting*. Skira, 2018.

This book features 80 paintings and drawings by Kerouac, most of which have never before been published, showing how he brought the same energy to visual art as he did to all of his other endeavors.

Hakutani, Yoshinobu. *Jack Kerouac and the Traditions of Classic and Modern Haiku*. Lexington Books, 2019.

Hakutani presents a reading of the haiku collected in Kerouac's *Book of Haikus*, edited by Regina Weinreich (2003), one of the two largest collections of English language haiku. Most of Kerouac's haiku reflect eastern philosophies—Confucianism, Buddhist ontology, and Zen—as do classic haiku, but Kerouac also conflates the Christian doctrine of mercy with that of Buddhism.

McClure, John A. "Vitalist Nation: Whitman, Kerouac, Rand, DeLillo." *Christianity and Literature*, vol. 67, no. 3, 2018.

This article describes romantic vitalism as a postsecular tradition of energy mysticism and traces its elaboration over the last two centuries. It identifies a tension in vitalist thinking, which can tend either toward unregulated self-assertion or toward the proposition that "everything that lives is holy" and deserving of respect. This tension emerges in Blake, Whitman, and Nietzsche, and it distinguishes Ayn Rand's *Atlas Shrugged* and Kerouac's *On the Road*.

Joanne Kyger

Soldosky, Adam. "'Those to Whom Interesting Things Happen': William Carlos Williams, Kenneth Rexroth, Lew Welch, and Joanne Kyger, and the Genome of San Francisco Renaissance Poetry." *William Carlos Williams Review*, vol. 35, no. 2, 2018.

This article examines the "genome" of the influence Williams's poetry has had in terms of its vernacular speech-based aesthetics on the poets of the San Francisco Renaissance. It argues that Williams's influence becomes a fixture in the evolution of Bay Area poets and poetics after this Renaissance and the ascendency of Beat poetry, through its continuation into the 1970s and 1980s.

Michael McClure

Nelson, Paul E. "Projective Verse: The Spiritual Legacy of the Beat Generation." See Melehy entry under Beat Generation.

Charles Olson

Byers, Mark. *Charles Olson and American Modernism: The Practice of the Self.* Oxford UP, 2018.

> This book draws on Olson's published and unpublished writings to establish an original account of early post-war American modernism. The development of Olson's work is seen to illustrate two primary drivers of formal innovation in the period: the evolution of a new model of political action pivoting around the radical individual and, relatedly, a powerful new critique of instrumental reason and the Enlightenment tradition.

Carbery, Matthew. *Phenomenology and the Late Twentieth-Century American Long Poem.* Palgrave Macmillan, 2019.

> This book reads major figures including Olson, Lyn Hejinian, Nathaniel Mackey, Susan Howe, and Rachel Blau DuPlessis within a new approach to the long poem tradition. It explores the ways in which American poets developed their poetic forms by engaging with a variety of European phenomenologists, including Hannah Arendt, Maurice Merleau-Ponty, Martin Heidegger, Emmanuel Levinas, and Jacques Derrida.

Hoeynck, Joshua. *Staying Open: Charles Olson's Sources and Influences.* Vernon Press, 2018.

> This edited collection of essays investigates inter-disciplinary influences on Olson's work, covering his engagement with the music of John Cage and Pierre Boulez, his interests in abstract expressionism, and his readings of philosopher Alfred North Whitehead. The essays also examine Olson's pedagogy, which he developed in the experimental environment at Black Mountain College, as well as his six-month archaeological journey through the Yucatan Peninsula in 1950 to explore the culture of the Maya. Building on the scholarship of George Butterick, whose guide to *The Maximus Poems* remains indispensable, the essays also help readers navigate the thick allusions within *The Maximus Poems* itself. The volume contains the following:

Clark, Dylan J. "An Archaeologist of Morning in the Mayab, 1951."

Davis, Jeff. "Shadow on the Rock: Morphology and Voice in Olson's Later *Maximus Poems.*"

Fineman, Daniel. "Olson, Peirce, Whitehead, and American Process Poetics."

Forrest, Johnson. "'Mu-sick mu-sick, mu-sick'": Olson's Stammer and the Poetics of Noise."

Gardner, Joshua. "Charles Olson and his 'Post-Modern' Exploration."

Hoeynck, Joshua. "Revising the Stane of 'Projective Verse': Charles Olsons' Ecological Vision of Alfred North Whitehead's Cosmology."

Jonik, Feff. "Olson's Poetics and Pedagogy: Influences at Black Mountain College."

Kindellan, Michael. "Projective Verse and Pedagogy."

Pree, Nathanael. "Maximus and Aboriginal Australia: Antipodean Influences on the Archaic Proprioceptive Epic."

Ruggeri, Alexander. "'By ear, he sd.': Open Listening with Charles Olson and John Cage."

Singer, Kirsty. "'What insides are': History—Gravitational and Unrelieved."

MacKay, Duncan. "If the Means are Equal: Charles Olson's Reciprocal Exchange." *PN Review*, vol. 44, no. 5, 2018.

Tedlock, Dennis. *The Olson Codex: Projective Verse and the Problem of Mayan Glyph.* UP of New Mexico, 2017.

This exploration of the influence of Mayan hieroglyphics on the American poet Charles Olson (1910-1970) is an important document in the history of New World verse. Olson spent six months in the Yucatan in 1951 studying Maya culture and language. Like Olson and Robert Creeley, who published Olson's letters from Mexico, the poet Dennis Tedlock taught at the University of Buffalo. Unlike his two predecessors, Tedlock was also a scholar of Maya language and culture, renowned for his translations from indigenous American languages, notably the Popul Vuh, the Maya creation story. In *The Olson Codex*, Tedlock describes and examines Olson's efforts to decipher Mayan hieroglyphics, giving Olson's work in Mexico a place within twentieth-century poetry and poetics.

Kenneth Rexroth

Soldosky, Adam. "'Those to Whom Interesting Things Happen': William Carlos Williams, Kenneth Rexroth, Lew Welch, and Joanne Kyger, and the Genome of San Francisco Renaissance Poetry." See entry under Kyger.

Lew Welch

Soldosky, Adam. "'Those to Whom Interesting Things Happen': William Carlos Williams, Kenneth Rexroth, Lew Welch, and Joanne Kyger, and the Genome of San Francisco Renaissance Poetry." See entry under Kyger.

Essay Abstracts

Jack Kerouac's Love Affair with Libraries
Le mal d'archive de Jack Kerouac
Jack Kerouac's Archive Fever
by Jean-Christophe Cloutier

This two-part essay, the first in French and the second an expanded English translation, explores Jack Kerouac's infatuation with libraries as part of his composition processes, necessary to a critical understanding of his Duluoz Legend. The essay traces his experiences as a young boy at the Pollard Public Library in Lowell, Massachusetts, through to his attempts as an adult to use the Bibliothèque Nationale in Paris, in the process exploring Kerouac's meticulous efforts to catalogue and archive his own literary works. Author Jean-Christophe Cloutier, translator of several of Kerouac's early texts orginially written in French (*The Unknown Kerouac* [2016]), draws on Kerouac's unpublished journals held in the Berg Collection of The New York Public Library as well as selections from the Duluoz Legend, including *Visions of Cody* (1972) and *Satori in Paris* (1966).

Virus and Word Virus: David Wojnarowicz, HIV/AIDS, and The Beat Generation
by Jonathan Sedberry

Through the lens of William S. Burroughs's worldview and Jack Kerouac's directives on spontaneous prose, this essay considers how mixed-media artist David Wojnarowicz's memoir, *Close to the Knives: A Memoir of Disintegration*, critiques and subverts the rhetoric responding to HIV/AIDS in the 1980s. In *Queer Burroughs*, Jamie Russell takes Burroughs to task for choosing to evade explicit recognition of the HIV/AIDS epidemic and the havoc it wrought in the American gay community of the 1980s and 1990s. However, decades spent employing art to combat social repression allowed Burroughs to contribute to the HIV/AIDS canon through influence, primarily through his impact on Wojnarowicz. Like Burroughs, Wojnarowicz recognized the limitations of language while paradoxically noting how language exists as a powerful mechanism through which to control. Burroughs's The Reality Studio becomes Wojnarowicz's "preinvented world" in which the idea of the ONE-TRIBE NATION dictates what is acceptable. In addition to borrowing and reimagining Burroughs's ideology and style, Wojnarowicz applied a style reflecting Kerouac's spontaneous prose to better express the emotion of the epidemic, especially as the underclasses experience it, and to develop a verbal x-ray to expose what lies behind the projected, preinvented world.

Notes on Contributors

Michael Amundsen holds a doctorate from the School of Humanities at Tallinn University, Estonia, where some of his work concerned looking at Jack Kerouac's writing for its ethnographic sensibilities. He has also written on busking culture, urban studies, and autoethnography as a research method. He is a journalist who has contributed to the Guardian, Financial Times, and many others. He is the editor of Baltic Publishing, an academic book publisher located in Tallinn, Estonia, and is co-editor of *Tallinn Arts* magazine. He is currently teaching at Arizona State University.

Jean-Christophe Cloutier originally hails from Beauport, Québec, and is assistant professor of English at the University of Pennsylvania. He received his doctorate from Columbia University where he also archived the papers of Samuel Roth, Erica Jong, and Barney Rosset. He is co-editor of Claude McKay's *Amiable with Big Teeth* (Penguin Classics, 2017), and editor of the original French writings of Jack Kerouac, *La vie est d'hommage* (Boréal, 2016). He also translated Kerouac's French novellas in the Library of America volume *The Unknown Kerouac: Rare, Unpublished & Newly Translated Writings* (2016). His book *Shadow Archives: The Lifecycles of African American Literature* is forthcoming from Columbia University Press (2019), and he is currently at work on an extensive study of Kerouac's oeuvre tentatively titled "Continenting Kerouac: Translation, Archive, Novel."

Maria Damon teaches in the Humanities and Media Studies and Writing departments at Pratt Institute of Art. She is the author of *The Dark End of the Street: Margins in American Poetry* (University of Minnesota Press, 1993), *Postliterary America: From Bagel Shop Jazz to Micropoetries* (University of Minnesota Press, 1993), and co-editor with Ira Livingston of *Poetry and Cultural Studies: A Reader* (University of Illinois Press, 2009).

Douglas Field is the co-founding editor of the *James Baldwin Review*, an annual peer-reviewed journal published by Manchester University Press, and a regular contributor to the *Times Literary Supplement*. He has published widely on Beat themes.

Chris Gair is senior lecturer in English and American Studies at the University of Glasgow. He is the author of *Complicity and Resistance in Jack London's Novels: From Naturalism to Nature* (Edwin Mellen Press, 1997), *The American Counterculture* (Edinburgh University Press, 2007), and *The Beat Generation: A Beginner's Guide* (One World Publications, 2012). He has published many essays and book chapters on American literature and culture, including, most recently, "'Thalatta, Thalatta!': Xenophon, Joyce and Kerouac" in *Hip Sublime: Beat Writers and the Classical Tradition* (The Ohio State Univerity Press, 2018).

Allan Johnston received his doctorate from the University of California Davis and teaches writing and literature at Columbia College–Chicago and DePaul University. He co-edits *JPSE: Journal for the Philosophical Study of Education* and has published studies of the Beats and other writers in *Twentieth Century Literature, College Literature, Review of Contemporary Fiction*, and others.

James Peacock is senior lecturer in English and American literatures at Keele University in the United Kingdom. His research focuses on contemporary American fiction, with a specific interest in New York novels, gentrification stories, transnational migration, and literary representations of neighborhood communities under globalization.

Jonathan Sedberry received his doctorate from the University of South Carolina in twentieth-century American and Commonwealth literatures, with a focus on literature of the HIV/AIDS epidemic. Currently working as an academic advisor for the College of Education at Georgia Southern University–Armstrong campus, he has taught literature, genre studies, and composition. He has presented papers on William S. Burroughs and Gregory Corso.

John Whalen-Bridge is associate professor of English at the National University of Singapore. Author of *Political Fiction and the American Self* (1998), he has co-edited (with Gary Storhoff) the SUNY series "Buddhism and American Culture." "Buddhism and the Beats" has appeared in *The Cambridge Companion to the Beats*. He is working on a study of engaged Buddhism and American writers, a biography of Maxine Hong Kingston, and a special issue of the *Journal of the Study of Religion, Nature, and Culture* focusing on religion, popular culture, and the Anthropocene.

Editorial Policy

The *Journal of Beat Studies* invites articles on the works of Beat movement writers and their colleagues, especially New York School, Black Mountain School, and San Francisco Renaissance writers, as well as those connected to these movements, in the United States and globally. The *Journal* intends to represent the breadth and eclecticism of critical approaches to Beat generation writers and welcomes new perspectives and contexts of inquiry.

Articles that are deemed appropriate are sent for review anonymously to a member of the Editorial Board and at least one other reader. Manuscripts should not be under consideration elsewhere, and we do not publish previously published work. It is strongly advised that those submitting work to *JBS* be familiar with the journal's content. Among criteria on which evaluation of submissions depends are whether an article demonstrates recognition of and thorough familiarity with scholarship already published in the field, whether the article is written clearly and effectively, and whether it makes a genuine contribution to Beat studies.

Preparation of Copy

1. Articles are typically between 25 and 30 pages, and do not exceed 9000 words, including notes and works cited. Inquiries about significantly shorter or longer submissions should be sent to the editors.

2. A separate page should include the article's title, author's name, address, telephone & fax numbers, e-mail address, and a 100-word professional biography. The author's name and identifying references should not appear on the manuscript to preserve anonymity for our readers.

3. All submissions must include an abstract of no more than 250 words.

4. The manuscript should be in Times New Roman 12, double-spaced, and should adhere to the most recent MLA style.

5. Submissions may be sent by email as word documents to Ronna C. Johnson (ronna.johnson@tufts.edu) and Nancy M. Grace (ngrace@wooster.edu) simultaneously. Mailed submissions should be sent to Ronna C. Johnson at Department of English, East Hall 102, The Green, Tufts University, Medford, Massachusetts 02155. For mailed submissions, please send three copies of the article and abstract.

6. Submissions may also be sent via the online submission form at http://www.beatstudies.org/jbs/submission_guidelines.html.

7. Authors of accepted manuscripts are responsible for any necessary permissions fees and for securing any necessary permissions.

8. All editorial and review inquiries should be addressed to ronna.johnson@tufts.edu and ngrace@wooster.edu.

9. Inquiries concerning orders and advertising exchanges should be addressed to PaceUP@pace.edu.

criticism
A Quarterly for Literature and the Arts

Jaime Goodrich, editor

Criticism provides a forum for current scholarship on literature, media, music, and visual culture. A place for rigorous theoretical and critical debate as well as formal and methodological self-reflexivity and experimentation, *Criticism* aims to present contemprary thought at its most vital.

Recent articles include

- The Permissible Narratives of Human Rights; or, how to be a Refugee
- Information Processing, Racial Semiotics, and Anti-Racist Protest, from "I am a Man" to "Black Lives Matter"
- The Desire for Fact: Anti-Racist Ethics in Discourses of Sexual Violence

For submission guidelines and subscription information, please visit http://digitalcommons.wayne.edu/criticism

Criticism is available in digital format to Project MUSE and JSTOR subscribers.

WAYNE STATE UNIVERSITY PRESS

The seventh volume of the *Journal of Beat Studies*
was published in Spring 2019
by Pace University Press

Cover and Interior Layouts by Jessica Estrella and Alicia Hughes
The journal was typeset in Times New Roman and AmerType Md BT
and printed by Lightning Source in La Vergne, Tennessee

Pace University Press

Director: Manuela Soares
Associate Director: Stephanie Hsu
Marketing Manager: Patricia Hinds
Design Consultant: Sara Yager
Production Editor: Stephanie Hsu

Graduate Assistants: Jessica Estrella and Alicia Hughes
Graduate Student Aide: Daren Fleming

www.ingramcontent.com/pod-product-compliance
Lightning Source LLC
Chambersburg PA
CBHW061419300426
44114CB00015B/1986